BREAD GROWS IN WINTER

IDA FRIEDERIKE GÖRRES

Bread Grows in Winter

With a eulogy by Joseph Ratzinger (Pope Benedict XVI)

TRANSLATED BY JENNIFER S. BRYSON

IGNATIUS PRESS SAN FRANCISCO

Original German edition:
Ida Friederike Görres,
Im Winter wächst das Brot. Sechs Versuche über die Kirche

Chapter 6 was published previously as Ida Friederike Görres, "Trusting the Church: A Lecture", *Logos* 23, no. 4 (Fall 2020): 123–47. The appendix was published previously as Joseph Ratzinger, "Eulogy for Ida Friederike Görres", *Logos* 23, no. 4 (Fall 2020): 148–51. The translator has edited the translations of chapter 6 and the appendix lightly for this book.

Cover design by Paweł Cetliński

ISBN 978-1-62164-738-6 (PB)
ISBN 978-1-64229-322-7 (eBook)
Library of Congress Control Number 2024950917
Printed in the United States of America ♾

This translation is dedicated to
"the hidden saints" of our era.

Contents

Foreword by Bishop Erik Varden 9
Translator's Introduction 11

1. Our Image of Christ: A Letter 43
2. Demolition Troops in the Church 71
3. Faith: Skeleton or Body? 85
4. The Spirituality of Studying Theology 95
5. Remarks on Celibacy 121
6. Trusting the Church 151

Appendix: "Eulogy for Ida Friederike Görres" 183
Register of Persons 189
Bibliography 195
Acknowledgments 209
Subject Index 211
Scripture Index 221

Foreword

I picked up a battered German copy of Ida Görres' *Bread Grows in Winter* from a junk shop years ago. This book, first published in 1970, has been a source of inspiration to me. During my first few years of episcopacy I often took it with me on journeys, as a travel companion. Trying to work out how to exercise the ministry, I found in Görres a sure guide unfailingly summoning me to focus on essentials.

Ida Görres was a woman of acute intelligence, able to fathom in herself great tensions. Her bicultural background kept her from simplifying questions of identity, cultural or ecclesiastical. When the Second Vatican Council began, she followed it enthusiastically. She remained committed to the Council's teaching, but was increasingly appalled by the crassness with which it was instrumentalized, here and there, as an excuse for mere deconstruction. She saw spiritual and intellectual treasures being thrown overboard as the bark of the Church made its way through choppy waters. This made her grieve both on her own behalf and on that of others.

Of course, she had read enough Church history to know that such losses are never final. There will always be pearl divers ready to descend to the bottom of the sea to fetch treasures up again, patiently removing strings of algae as they rejoice in sharing their finds. But why go to such trouble when a peaceful handing-on (in Latin, a *traditio*) in view of present mission and future growth remains an option?

It would be a mistake to present Ida Görres as just an antiquarian. Her concern was theological. She insisted, as had the Council Fathers in their constitution *Lumen gentium*, that the Church must be understood as a sacramental, personal reality. Görres regretted the eclipse of theology in much that was said about the Church, and done to her in consequence, in the heady years of the late 1960s, with the West caught up in a cultural revolution that unfolded, often enough, as a targeted assault on institutions. The Church, she kept repeating, can neither be rightly understood nor truly loved by one who regards her in institutional terms while failing to recognize her as "the strangest creation of God, so unique in kind, so large, so contradictory, so colorful that no single person can take stock of her and figure her out, and certainly no outsider can ever take her all in, let alone understand her and judge her".[1]

For much too long, the theology of Ida Görres has been a minority interest passed on among initiates who recognize each other, as it were, by way of secret handshakes or knowing looks. I rejoice that these boundaries are bursting. The publication of Görres' work in English is a major event full of promise for the Church's mission, at once ancient and ever new, "to carry forward the work of Christ under the lead of the befriending Spirit".[2]

Most Rev. Erik Varden
Bishop of Trondheim, Norway

[1] See p. 162.

[2] Pastoral Constitution on the Church in the Modern World *Gaudium et spes* (December 7, 1965), no. 3.

Translator's Introduction

In 1969 and again in 1970, Ida Friederike Görres described the situation in the Church as a "crisis". She did so first in her 1969 article "Demolition Troops in the Church", chapter 2 in this volume, and then in her 1970 lecture "Trusting the Church", chapter 6 in this volume.[1] In his eulogy at her funeral in 1971, Father Joseph Ratzinger (later Pope Benedict XVI) also described the era as a "crisis".[2] Görres knew she was not alone in her alarm. "I speak", she said in the same lecture in 1970, "on behalf of many who remain silent or are at a loss for words."[3] She asked, "What is still firm and tranquil today in the Church, in Christianity, in our faith? What does not waver and wobble? What is not being challenged from the outside and, most harshly, from the inside?"[4] Those questions are as relevant today as they were when Görres first published and delivered the four essays and two lectures contained in *Bread Grows in Winter.*

In these six chapters, Görres does not mince words. We read of "demolition troops",[5] as well as "destruction and betrayal".[6] For many of her contemporaries and, during some moments, for Görres herself, the Church was beginning to

[1] Chapter 2, p. 71, and chapter 6, p. 151.

[2] Appendix, p. 186.

[3] Chapter 6, p. 151.

[4] Chapter 6, p. 153.

[5] Chapter 2, p. 71.

[6] Chapter 6, p. 161.

appear less a City on the Hill than an institution perched precariously on the edge of a raging ocean, with wave after wave trying to break through the dams and levees the Church so carefully put into place to protect herself over nearly two thousand years. It looked, at times, as if the Church might even be dismantling parts of her own protective structures.

Yet, alongside writing bluntly about horror stories of "demolition" and "destruction", Görres shows her troubled readers what is "still firm and tranquil",[7] and she draws on this to shine a light for them—and for us today—on the heart of the Church. She even voices a hope for the future that we are indeed starting to see today; writing of a counterpart to those engaging in the "destruction", she muses, "Maybe their grandchildren—out of generational contrariety!—will have had enough of trampling and rejection and will extract great discoveries from that which is defamed and withheld from them today."[8]

"We must be satisfied", she said in her 1970 lecture, "with the knowledge that the City on the Hill is still there behind the fog that makes it invisible to many. . . . We must be able to wait through snowmelt and flood, and even starless nights, knowing that stars are more enduring than clouds."[9] Yes, even on nights when "fog" and "clouds" obscure the "stars", Görres helps us to see that we can have confidence that the "stars" are still there, just waiting for the next opportunity to shine light into darkness.

[7] Chapter 6, p. 153.
[8] Chapter 6, p. 180.
[9] Chapter 6, p. 180.

Ida Friederike Görres
(née von Coudenhove-Kalergi)

Ida Friederike Görres (1901–1971) was a Catholic author whose works were well known during her lifetime in German-speaking Europe and elsewhere as well through translations, especially into English and Dutch.[10] She was the daughter of a Habsburg Empire diplomat and his Japanese wife, whom he met while he was stationed in Tokyo. Görres was born and grew up on the family estate in Bohemia. She attended convent boarding schools starting at age eleven and later began her university studies in Austria; she later continued (though did not complete) her studies in Germany. She was raised Catholic, but it was only after a conversion experience at age fifteen while in boarding school with the Mary Ward Sisters that her faith became central to her life. She spent two years in a convent in Austria as a novice but discerned that she should pursue a different path. Afterward, she became active in the Catholic Youth Movement in the 1920s and '30s, at first in Austria and then more intensely in Germany; this was a transformative period in her life. In the 1920s, she began to publish her written work, mostly in prominent Catholic journals associated with the Catholic Youth Movement. From 1932 until she married in 1935, she led lay ministry for girls and women in Dresden. At

[10] For information about the translation of Görres' works into other languages, see Jennifer Sue Bryson, "The Reception of Ida Friederike Görres in English from 1932 to 2022" and "Ida Friederike Görres in Translation 1932–2022: A Bibliography in Fourteen Languages", in *"Glut und Schmerz des Glaubens": Ein neuer Blick auf Ida Friederike Görres (1901–1971)*, eds. Hanna-Barbara Gerl-Falkovitz and Sigmund Bonk (Regensburg: Verlag Friedrich Pustet, 2023), 190–211 and 212–23, respectively.

the same time, translation of her works into English began, published by Sheed and Ward and, later, Longmans, Green & Co.[11]

She and her husband, Carl-Josef, were unable to have children, and this was a source of great pain in her life. Her life's work, her fruitfulness in addition to being a wife, became her writing. As for so many writers, the publication of her work was largely (though not entirely) interrupted by World War II while she continued working on books and essays. In the mid- to late 1940s, she published a flurry of works and resumed speaking at Catholic events. She occupied an unusual position as a lay Catholic author (and a woman) who was outside academic circles while a respected, even if at times controversial, Catholic writer in German-speaking Europe.

In his eulogy at her funeral in 1971, Ratzinger acknowledged her uniqueness and what he called the "periods of blackout in the past few years" in the Church—that is, the situation addressed by Görres in this book.[12] He said that, with the death of Görres, "a voice has been taken away from us, a voice which seems irreplaceable to the Church in this situation, when we are in a desert of conformism

[11] Her works translated into English in the 1930s are these: Ida Friederike Coudenhove, "The Nature of Sanctity: A Dialogue", in *The Persistence of Order: Essays on Religion and Culture*, ed. T. F. Burns and Christopher Dawson, trans. Ruth Bonsall and Edward Watkin, 1:125–96 (Providence: Cluny Media, 2019), first published by Sheed and Ward in 1932; Ida Friederike Coudenhove, *The Burden of Belief*, with an introduction by Gerald Vann, trans. Conrad Mario Ricco Bonacina (London: Sheed and Ward, 1934); Ida Friederike Coudenhove, *The Cloister and the World*, trans. Harriet Eleanor Kennedy (London: Sheed and Ward, 1935); Ida Friederike Görres, *Mary Ward*, trans. Elsie Codd (London: Longmans, Green, 1938).

[12] "Eulogy", p. 185.

or embarrassed silence."[13] He continued, "She spoke with an insightful certainty and a fearlessness about the pressing questions and tasks of the Church today, something which is given only to the one who truly believes."[14]

Görres wrote on many topics, always informed by her love of the Church and her deep faith. The nature of sanctity and the lives of the saints formed the core of her work. Today, she is best known for her important biography of Saint Thérèse of Lisieux, *The Hidden Face.*[15] She also published books and many essays on the Church, ethical-social issues, and the Catholic faith.[16] In Görres' lifelong career as a writer, short-form essays, long-form essays, and occasionally published lectures, such as those in this book, were a mainstay of her work. She published these individually in journals and together in anthologies. In addition, she published poetry, plays, three dialogues,[17] and several of her book-length works were collections of epistolary essays, a genre we will see in chapter 1 of this book.[18]

[13] "Eulogy", p. 184.

[14] "Eulogy", p. 184.

[15] Ida Friederike Görres *The Hidden Face: A Study of Saint Thérèse of Lisieux*, trans. Richard and Clara Winston (1959; San Francisco: Ignatius Press, 2003).

[16] Görres' best-known work on the Church is her book *The Church in the Flesh*, trans. Jennifer S. Bryson (Providence: Cluny Media, 2023; first published in German in 1950).

[17] Ida Friederike Coudenhove, "The Nature of Sanctity: A Dialogue", in *Essays on Religion and Culture*, eds. T. F. Burns and Christopher Dawson, trans. Ruth Bonsall and Edward Watkin, 1:125–96; Ida Friederike Görres, *The Persistence of Order* (Providence: Cluny Media, 2019); Ida Friederike Coudenhove, *The Burden of Belief*, trans. Conrad Mario Ricco Bonacina (London: Sheed & Ward, 1934); Ida Friederike Görres, *Des andern Last: Ein Gespräch über die Barmherzigkeit* (Freiburg im Breisgau: Herder, 1940).

[18] For example, her collections of letters include these: Coudenhove, *The Cloister and the World*; Ida Friederike Görres, *Von Ehe und von Einsamkeit: Ein Beitrag in vier Briefen* (Donauwörth, Germany: Cassianeum, 1949),

Chapters 1–6 and the Eulogy: Background and Key Themes

The German edition of *Bread Grows in Winter* does not identify where or when these six chapters originated. However, I was able to find information about the background of five of the six chapters as well as the appendix, which I present below. This information is based on other works by Görres, secondary sources, and letters Görres wrote to Father Paulus Gordan, O.S.B., from the 1960s until her death in 1971.[19] These letters were a particularly fruitful source of information; the translations of selections from these letters in this introduction are my own. Also, I highlight central themes of each chapter and identify how some of these themes relate to similar topics in Görres' other works.

---

forthcoming in English as *On Marriage and on Being Single*, trans. Jennifer S. Bryson, and Görres, *The Church in the Flesh*.

[19] I relied most of all on a nearly comprehensive bibliography of Görres' works prepared by Father Michael Kleinert for his dissertation on Ida Görres in 2001 and the letters written by Görres to Paulus Gordan, O.S.B., from 1962 to 1971. Michael Kleinert, *Es wächst viel Brot in der Winternacht: Theologische Grundlinien im Werk von Ida Friederike Görres*, vol. 36 of Studien zur systematischen und spirituellen Theologie (Würzburg: Echter, 2002), 389–411. Ida Friederike Görres, *"Wirklich die neue Phönixgestalt?": Über Kirche und Konzil; Unbekannte Briefe 1962–1971 von Ida Friederike Görres an Paulus Gordan*, ed. Hanna-Barbara Gerl-Falkovitz (Heiligenkreuz im Wienerwald, Austria: Be+Be Verlag, 2015). (The letters from Gordan to Görres, as well as letters to Görres from others, such as Joseph Ratzinger and Hans Urs von Balthasar, plus some of her papers, are in the archives of the Archdiocese of Freiburg, Germany; I did not have access to these while writing this introduction.)

Chapter 1. Our Image of Christ: A Letter

"Our Image of Christ: A Letter" was first published in 1968 by itself as a monograph in Germany.[20] In it, Görres responds to the concerns of an apparently semifictional reader that the image Catholics have had of Christ for centuries is being swept away by the zeitgeist. Görres steps back and helps her correspondent view both Christ and His Church from a broad perspective, not least of all a perspective that extends temporally beyond whatever the latest scandalous remarks about Christ may be. Skillfully guiding her readers to reposition their perspective to see the big picture, as she does here, is a common feature in Görres' work.

Another common feature in her work was that she had a sensitive finger on the pulse of the laity. One sees this, for example, in her famous "Letter on the Church" in 1946, her book *The Church in the Flesh* in 1950, and in this essay "Our Image of Christ".[21] Her choice of the literary genre of a "letter", that is, an epistolary essay, to address the concerns of her interlocutor, reflects a sense of

[20] Ida Friederike Görres, "Zu unserem Christus Bild: Ein Brief", in *Unphilosophische Brocken* 2 (1968).

[21] Ida Friederike Görres, "A Letter on the Church", *Dublin Review* 223, no. 446 (Winter 1949): 71–89; Ida Friederike Görres, *The Church in the Flesh*, trans. Jennifer S. Bryson (Providence: Cluny Media, 2023).

This English edition of "A Letter on the Church" is identified in the *Dublin Review* as "adapted and translated" (p. iv); it is, in fact, largely "adapted". The English text captures the spirit of the original German text very well. In the details, however, it is somewhat loose at times, and several entire paragraphs are missing. The full version can be found in German in Ida Friederike Görres, "Brief über die Kirche", *Frankfurter Hefte* 1, no. 8 (1946): 715–33. I have prepared a new, complete translation of "A Letter on the Church" with an introduction about the origins and impact of this famous essay for a forthcoming book.

emotional connection with him. This chapter is likely not an actual letter from Görres' correspondence; it may be, but it is more likely a composite, semifictional letter to address the concerns of many with whom she corresponded and whom she met in various situations. Her use of the personal tone of a letter addressed to an individual provided her a way to connect with her readers, whose concerns were so well known to her, and to let them know their concerns were heard.

Letters, in addition to having a personal tone, also served as a proxy, as a way for her to engage in "conversation" with those whom she could not meet in person. Görres cherished conversations. Her friend Alfons Rosenberg explained:

> Although Ida Görres presents herself to the world as a writer, her writing emerges from the spoken word—she is decidedly a person for whom conversation is paramount. That is why, even if not always externally recognizable, her writings are mostly created as dialogues, either explicitly or in letters with distant and invisible partners. She always speaks in an engaging manner and prompts a response.[22]

Rosenberg added, "Only when one meets with Ida Görres for a conversation, which she tirelessly likes best of all to stretch out over many hours, does one feel the full strength of who she is."[23] And her essays in the form of "letters" were not just a one-way conversation. She also received letters from her readers. While she corresponded with some of them, her epistolary essays, like the one in chapter 1 of this book, served as a sort of collective response.

The personal nature of a letter also reflects the keen pastoral sensitivity one sees throughout the work of Ida Görres;

[22] Alfons Rosenberg, "A Panoramic View of Ida Friederike Görres", in Görres, *The Church in the Flesh*, xv.

[23] Rosenberg, "A Panoramic View", xv.

she always had a concern for the souls of the people in the pew. Thus, her use of the form of a letter with a personal tone reflects her hope to reach not only the minds but also the hearts and, most importantly, the souls of her readers.

Several personal touches in this "letter" suggest that there is a specific addressee. For example, Görres opens the letter by quoting from a letter she has received (a common pattern in her epistolary essays). And toward the end of the letter, in a passage about Catholic priests, she writes, "You know this, your brother is also among them." At any rate, the "letter" in chapter 1 is meant to be read as a letter to you, the reader; the addressee should be understood as "My dear Catholic friend".[24] We do not know whether chapter 1 started out as an actual letter and then developed into an essay for publication or whether the entire letter was crafted for publication. The personal elements are either remnants from one or several initial actual letters or finishing touches, added to give the reader a more intimate experience in reading this letter.

Chapter 2. Demolition Troops in the Church

"Demolition Troops in the Church" was first published in the newspaper *Die Presse* (The Press) in Vienna in the weekend supplement of March 29–30, 1969, at the start of Holy Week.[25]

The jarring nature of the English title, "Demolition Troops in the Church", is also present in the original German title,

[24] On Görres' use of letters as a literary genre, see also Jennifer S. Bryson, "Translator's Note", in Görres, *The Church in the Flesh*, xxvii, xxix–xxx.

[25] Ida Friederike Görres, "Abbruchkommandos in der Kirche: Der Katholizismus zwischen den Kräften der Zerstörung und der Rodung für eine neue Zeit", *Die Presse*, Weekend Supplement, March 29–30, 1969.

"Abbruchkommandos in der Kirche". The full title of the original essay when first published in *Die Presse* was "Demolition Troops in the Church: Catholicism between the Forces of Destruction and Clearing the Way for a New Era". This title was shortened to "Demolition Troops in the Church" when the essay was republished in *Bread Grows in Winter.*

Görres' use of martial language in the title of chapter 2 is intentional. In this chapter, we also see martial terms such as "fratricidal war", "enemies", "camouflage", and "revolution". And as can be seen under the category "warfare" in the index of this book, martial language is found throughout these six chapters. I believe this reflects how seriously Görres considered the stakes of the fighting in the Church. This may also reflect her recognition of the reality of spiritual warfare. She had, for example, a strong devotion to Saint Michael the Archangel and included an image of him on her gravestone.

Görres was aware that the content of this essay was bold. She even wondered if it might be *too* bold for the editors of *Die Presse.* In a letter to her friend Father Paulus Gordan on March 28, 1968, Görres writes, "I am fiddling with my commentary that has been commissioned on the concluding documents of the Council, which I now have in their entirety in front of me." In her next letter to Gordan, on April 7, 1968, she continues, "I am sending you two mss. [manuscripts] enclosed just for reading, *no hurry at all*! One is the commentary on the final documents of the Council commissioned from Vienna. I am very curious whether the editors will accept it!"[26]

[26] Görres, *Wirklich die neue Phönixgestalt?*, 336. Mss. = manuscripts. The editor of this collection of letters with Gordan, Gerl-Falkovitz, suggests that

A year later, on March 21, 1969, Görres writes to Gordan:

> On the other hand, for various reasons, both pious and worldly, one cannot stop writing short essays—and one's competence to do so feels endlessly questionable. "According to your words you will be judged"[27]—there's that too. In this regard, I'm terribly busy, with one writing assignment after another. Yesterday, a long essay was sent "express-registered", as they say at the post office, to the—would you believe?—Easter week supplement of *Die Presse* in Vienna. What was once the *Neue Freie Presse* . . . is now, to my enormous astonishment, decently Catholic, perhaps conservative—I'm not even sure. Dr. Otto Schulmeister, the former editor in chief of *Wort und Wahrheit*, is there now. He wrote to me about this around New Year's Day. And I actually did it only because he is such an immensely decent person who stays there with really admirable, *completely* disillusioned loyalty, simply because, as he wrote, we shouldn't be mute dogs and disappear into the bushes as so many people are now doing in the Church as well as in politics. On top of this, the essay is about the Church crisis!!
>
> I find it hard to resist such an appeal—although I've never written anything in my life for a daily newspaper supplement and have no idea how to do so, since I don't read any.
>
> . . . H U v [Hans Urs von] Balthasar, with whom I am now in a *very* peculiar relationship because of his Adrienne,[28] recently wrote to me: "Don't work too hard. In spite of all our

---

the "commentary" mentioned here by Görres was "Demolition Troops in the Church", 336n471.

[27] See Mt 7:2.

[28] "Adrienne" refers to Adrienne von Speyr, with whom Hans Urs von Balthasar had a very close relationship. Görres had an ambiguous view of Adrienne von Speyr. See, for example, her letters to Father Paulus Gordan on November 4, 1968, and November 28, 1968, in *"Wirklich die neue Phönixgestalt?"*, 389–90 and 397–98, respectively.

> efforts, we already belong to a forgotten generation." Certainly. But that does not seem to me to be a reason. I still have energy for short essays—and didn't Mother Teresa, the saint of Calcutta, tell me almost a year ago: "Write for the common people; tell them what the Council really wanted; help them keep the faith during this confusion"? Now this has fallen into place for me on its own.
>
> . . . And actually, you also aren't doing anything other than this, just on a different level. It seems as if it's a contemporary calling.[29]

In a postscript to a letter to Gordan on May 8, 1969, Görres asked, "I wonder if you liked my 'Demolition' [essay]?"[30]

This essay, beginning right from its startling title, no doubt ruffled some feathers. Yet Görres was no stranger to controversy. Her 1946 essay "A Letter on the Church" stirred up a hornet's nest in the German Church, and she paid a significant price for raising her voice as she did.[31] For example, Cardinal Michael von Faulhaber banned Görres from public speaking in his Archdiocese of Munich and Freising after the essay was published. She had severe health problems in the following years, likely bearing a connection to this backlash. The entire episode following the publication of "A Letter on the Church" is largely what Ratzinger is referring to when, in his eulogy, he discusses how this woman who so loved the Church had to deal with times when "the Church . . . appeared to be her own opponent".[32] Yet, her

[29] *"Wirklich die neue Phönixgestalt?"*, 416–18. *Wort und Wahrheit* (Word and truth) was a monthly journal on religion and culture, Catholic and somewhat academic, published in Austria from 1946 to 1973.

[30] *"Wirklich die neue Phönixgestalt?"*, 413.

[31] Ida Friederike Görres, "A Letter on the Church", trans. Ida Friederike Görres, *Dublin Review* 223, no. 446 (Winter 1949): 71–89.

[32] "Eulogy", p. 185.

recognition of malaise and alienation simmering under the surface in the Church in Germany in 1946 proved more accurate than many were willing to admit at the time. More recently, writers such as Peter Seewald, in his 2020 biography of Ratzinger, have recognized how prescient Görres' insights in 1946 were.[33] And the late 1960s, as the editor of the newspaper wrote to her, were not a time to "disappear into the bushes". Görres was hardly one to do so; she loved the Church too much to remain silent amid trouble and suffering in the Church.

"Demolition Troops in the Church" provides readers with a window on how much upheaval and "destruction" were already underway in the Church following the Second Vatican Council, even prior to the dramatic changes introduced by the *Novus ordo Missae*, the New Order of the Mass, in 1969–1970. We know from previous works that Görres was well aware of, and critical regarding, far-reaching experimentation underway in the liturgy earlier in the 1960s.[34] When, however, she was writing this essay—which we know, from her correspondence with Gordan, goes back a full year to 1968—she did not yet see the Novus Ordo, in particular, coming. She remarked in this essay that the liturgy "has not yet been forced into line with being just a matter for a commission!" As we now know, this was changing as well. The Novus Ordo was promulgated on April 3, 1969, a few days after this essay was published.

Aside from Görres' commentary on the drama of the era,

[33] Peter Seewald, *Benedict XVI: A Life*, trans. Dinah Livingstone, vol. 1, *Youth in Nazi Germany to the Second Vatican Council 1927–1965* (London: Bloomsbury Continuum, 2020), 326, 328.

[34] See, for example, Ida Friederike Görres, "When Does a Person Have a Capacity for Liturgy?" trans. Jennifer S. Bryson, *Logos* 25, no. 3 (Summer 2022): 126–39.

"Demolition Troops in the Church" is also noteworthy for her evocative analogies and rich descriptions of nature. We read of the complexity and necessity of the many parts and phases of a stunning flower (the whole plant, she emphasizes, not just the grand bloom!), and there is a powerful description of tidal flooding and the important role of manmade dams and levees. Görres was a very keen observer of nature, and her writings are filled with detailed, often beautiful descriptions and images from the natural world.[35]

Chapter 3. Faith: Skeleton or Body?

Whether Görres published the third essay, "Faith: Skeleton or Body?", prior to its publication in *Bread Grows in Winter* is unknown.

In this essay, Görres explains her concern that the pendulum of theological discussions in the Church had swung from being "finicky pedantry and, combined with policing methods, . . . also a serious stumbling block for theological development within the Church", to having an absence of any "boundaries and distinctions".[36] This absence fosters not breadth but shallowness: Görres calls it "a 'naked' theology . . . with itself as the supreme authority of faith. . . .

[35] To mention just one of many examples, see her rich descriptions of the landscape, the plants, and the dynamic change of seasons in the region around Heiligenkreuz im Wienerwald in Austria in her short story "The Bride of Alexius": Ida Friederike Görres, "Die Braut des Alexis", in *Die Braut des Alexis und andere Mädchengeschichten* (Freiburg im Breisgau: Herder, 1949), 261–93. I have translated this story into English (forthcoming). See also the introduction to this story: Jennifer Sue Bryson, "Leselicht: Eine unabsehbare Wechselwirkung von menschlicher und göttlicher Liebe" in *Neue Schau: Große christliche Erzählungen im 20.* Jahrhundert, eds. Hanna-Barbara Gerl-Falkovitz and Gudrun Trausmuth, Kleine Bibliothek des Abendlandes (Heiligenkreuz im Wienerwald, Austria: Be+Be-Verlag, 2023), 9:191–98.

[36] "Skeleton or Body?", p. 87.

It is a skeleton without a body, and not even a whole skeleton."[37]

While Görres finds both extremes of the pendulum problematic—excessive inflexibility and revolution—it is the latter she views as a setting for heresy (or even schism). In this chapter, she asks, "Is there, one asks oneself, still a binding norm of orthodoxy, even for the responsible guardians of the truths of the faith? Current theological activity does not exactly thrust this impression onto an observer. The silence of the Magisterium dismays the faithful, who are facing the merrily rampant spread of heresies of all shades."[38] She contrasts them with her experience during the Catholic Youth Movement in the 1920s, in which "tradition and history" played a vital role "for personal and ecclesial renewal", and they were valued "for the whole, within the whole".[39]

She concludes on a note of hope, describing "the true heirs, the shapers of tomorrow's Church, the spokespersons for her future"; she says that even in such turmoil as there was at the time, "they already exist."[40] Expressing the broad view so characteristic of her work, she notes that they will be "connected to their predecessors by lineage and by Tradition that cannot be broken" while being "not just a defensive rearguard".[41]

Chapter 4. The Spirituality of Studying Theology

Görres originally delivered "The Spirituality of Studying Theology" as a lecture in 1967. Next, she published it in

[37] "Skeleton or Body?", p. 90.
[38] "Skeleton or Body?", p. 86.
[39] "Skeleton or Body?", p. 88.
[40] "Skeleton or Body?", p. 94.
[41] "Skeleton or Body?", p. 94.

a Festschrift in 1968 before including it in *Bread Grows in Winter* in 1970.[42]

In the letter to Gordan on April 7, 1968, mentioned earlier, in which Görres wrote that she was sending him two manuscripts; the second manuscript appears to have been this essay.[43] She wrote in that letter:

> The second is the talk I gave last year here in St. Ulrich at the retreat for the lay theology students, as a stopgap for someone prominent who dropped out, that is, for Hans Urs von Balthasar. Now I have released the essay to be printed in a Festschrift (i.e., a mass grave)[44] for Fr. Viktor Schurr, C.Ss.R., in Gars, for his seventieth birthday. He did me a great service a dozen years ago (unfortunately, nothing came of it—he got me two suitcases of Brentano diaries about A. C. Emmerich from Rome, which I wanted to work on

[42] Ida Friederike Görres, "Eine Besinnung über die Spiritualität des Theologie-studiums", in *Wort in Welt: Studien zur Theologie der Verkündigung; Festgabe für Viktor Schurr*, ed. Wolfdieter Theurer (Bergen-Enkheim bei Frankfurt am Main: Kaffke, 1968), 272–84.

[43] In a footnote to this letter, Gerl-Falkovitz suggests this may have been Görres' essay "Maria war damals die ganze Kirche", published in February 1968, but the essay Görres mentions in the next sentence for the Festschrift for Viktor Schurr is "The Spirituality of Studying Theology". *"Wirklich die neue Phönixgestalt?"*, 336–37; see footnote 472. (The essay suggested by Gerl-Falkovitz is Ida Friederike Görres, "Maria war damals die ganze Kirche", *Freiburger Artikel- und Redaktionsdienst* 12, no. 18 [1968]: 2–3.)

[44] Görres was joking when she wrote that a Festschrift is like a "mass grave". Festschrifts, which gather essays published in honor of a scholar (most common) or a prominent writer such as Görres, usually have only a small print run and quickly fall into obscurity. A case in point is the Festschrift for Ida Görres' sixtieth birthday. Even after I had been translating Görres' works for almost two years, I was unaware of the existence of this Festschrift until Hanna-Barbara Gerl-Falkovitz gave me a copy as a gift in 2021. At the time, she remarked, "There are very few copies of this; it is hard to come by." Its publisher has gone out of business. This Festschrift was indeed a sort of "mass grave" for essays by significant Catholic writers, such as Rosenberg and Gustav Siewerth. See Alfons Rosenberg, ed., *Wanderwege. Festschrift Zum 60: Geburtstag von Ida Friederike Görres* (Zurich: Thomas Verlag, 1961).

> at that time, but I was too ill; nothing came out) and so I could not easily refuse to take part.[45]

By "here in St. Ulrich" she likely means at the monastery of St. Ulrich in Bollschweil, Germany, near Freiburg. She and her husband, Carl-Josef, lived in Freiburg at the time.

This essay highlights two features of Görres' work. One is that, while she was highly learned and well read, she was not an academic. This gave her intellectual independence from the powerful currents that at times fostered an echo chamber among some university and seminary professors. In this essay, she has enough distance to be critical of these trends. Second, here again we see how her work is imbued, as throughout her lifetime, with a keen pastoral sensitivity. This finds expression in her understanding of and concern for the "ordinary Christians" ("the people in the pews", as she calls them in another essay).[46]

Görres argued that the study of theology needs to include not just intellectual ideas but

> *love for the listener*, love for the unlearned, the simple, the "ordinary Christians", who, unfortunately, so often appear to the learned theologians only as a disdained object to be taught and "enlightened". Are they not to be understood as the "poor of Christ" just as much as the materially poor? . . . Even a thimble filled to the brim is still full. It is better to help them to reach such fullness in their own language than to baffle and confuse them and tug at their roots with an accoutrement of unintelligible foreign words.

[45] *"Wirklich die neue Phönixgestalt?"*, 336–37. C.Ss.R. = Congregation of the Most Holy Redeemer. A. C. Emmerich = Anne Catherine Emmerich.

[46] "Capacity for Liturgy", 134.

Chapter 5. Remarks on Celibacy

Görres first published "Remarks on Celibacy" or part of it in 1969 in Germany as a monograph.[47] In addition, she published an excerpt in a journal called *Die Sendung* under the title "Remarks about Celibacy", and she published part of section 2 in the Austrian weekly *Die Furche* and in the German weekly *Rheinischer Merkur* under the headline "Overemphasis on the Masculine in the Church Drives Flight from 'Mother' Church."[48]

Görres had previously written a short book on celibacy, first published in German in 1962.[49] This book contains two long essays—one on the priesthood and one on relations between priests and women. It was translated into five languages, including English in 1965, published as *Is Celibacy Outdated?*[50]

Addressing the issue of priestly celibacy, a hotly contested topic in the 1960s, Görres argues in "Remarks on Celibacy" that the reason her contemporaries did not understand it is that they did not understand the priesthood itself. The title of this essay in the German edition is simply "Remarks about

[47] Ida Friederike Görres, "Bemerkungen zum Zölibat", *Unphilosophische Brocken* 4 (1969).

[48] Ida Friederike Görres, "Bemerkungen zum Zölibatstreit", *Die Sendung* 23 (1970), 17–21; Ida Friederike Görres, "Überbetonung des Maskulinen drängt in der Kirche Flucht vor der 'Mutter' Kirche," *Die Furche*, August 9, 1969, 9; Ida Friederike Görres, "Flucht vor der 'Mutter' Kirche," *Rheinischer Merkur*, July 11, 1969.

[49] Ida Friederike Görres, *Laiengedanken zum Zölibat* (Frankfurt am Main, Germany: Knecht Verlag, 1962).

[50] Ida Friederike Görres, *Is Celibacy Outdated?*, trans. Barbara Waldstein-Wartenberg (Westminster, Md.: Newman Press, 1965). The other four translations were into Dutch, French, Portuguese, and Slovenian; see Bryson, "Görres in Translation", 215, 219, 222, 223; "Translations", Ida Friederike Görres, last visited May 28, 2025, https://www.idagoerres.org/translations.

Celibacy" ("Bemerkungen zum Zölibat"); given the content of this chapter, Görres could have titled it "Remarks about Celibacy and Confusion about the Priesthood". In typical Görres fashion, she shows readers the need to step back from the specific issue—in this case, celibacy—and look at the topic in its entirety, from a broad perspective, in the context of the Church. She argues that to understand why there is so much skepticism about celibacy, one needs to see that the roots of this confusion lie in a broader confusion about what the priesthood is.

In her essay, we read about some of the proposals in vogue in the 1960s—and even already in the 1830s—such as turning the priesthood into a part-time gig, with lawyers, doctors, and other professionals just celebrating Mass on the side on Sundays. Görres granted that, in a priesthood viewed as the aspiring reformers saw it, it would make sense that celibacy would not be an essential component. However, explained Görres, *just another job* is precisely what the priesthood is not.

Görres situated celibacy itself within broader contexts, explaining its relationship to sacrifice and human sex as well as the dynamic relation between men and women; these are themes she developed in other works as well.[51] Görres

[51] For example, she explains how understanding the role of sacrifice can help give meaning to the lives of those who want to marry but remain single for various reasons. See chapters 2 and 3 of Ida Friederike Gorres, *On Marriage and on Being Single*, trans. Jennifer S. Bryson (forthcoming). She wrote two books on marriage: in 1949, the one just mentioned, and in 1971, Ida Friederike Görres, *What Binds Marriage Forever*, trans. Jennifer S. Bryson (Washington, D.C.: Catholic University of America Press, 2025). As the sexual revolution began to unfold in the twentieth century, she fired warning flares in the 1950s and 1960s, writing in her published journals and in essays on topics as varied as the falsehoods of feminism, the risks of interfaith marriage, the trend toward the breakdown of marriage, the harms of contraception, and the dangers as well as the repugnancy of artificial reproduction.

understood sex, and with it, virginity, as a very deep part of culture, society, and civilization, as well as of the human person. The interrelated topics of marriage, virginity, chastity, and celibacy appear in many of her works. A reason she used her role as a writer to defend the *depth* and *breadth* of traditional Catholic teachings on sex and virginity is that she saw each as having a unique capacity to communicate profound truths about human beings. This includes, importantly, metaphysical aspects of these truths.[52]

Chapter 6. Trusting the Church

"Trusting the Church" is the text of a lecture Görres delivered in Badenweiler, Germany, on April 17, 1970.[53] The lecture was first published in the German edition of this book in 1970. A month after her death in 1971, an excerpt of it was republished under the title, "'Angels and devils have been abolished': Still Trusting the Church?" in the Austrian weekly newspaper *Die Furche*.[54]

In this lecture, Görres depicts the rapid implosion of Catholic tradition in Germany, and the Netherlands too, in the wake of the Second Vatican Council and the introduction

[52] An example of the importance Görres placed on the metaphysical significance of man and woman can be seen in one of her many criticisms of Simone de Beauvoir's book *The Second Sex* and the notion of "woman" de Beauvoir advances. Görres argues that Beauvoir's reduction of woman to being just "a 'neutral working animal with female genital organs' " reduces her to something "metaphysically completely 'mute' ". Ida Friederike Görres, " 'Satanic' and 'An Atheistic Doctrine of Woman': A Review of Simone de Beauvoir's *The Second Sex* (1951)", trans. Jan C. Bentz and Jennifer S. Bryson, *Interpretation: A Journal of Political Philosophy* 49, no. 3 (Spring 2023): 411–22.

[53] *"Wirklich die neue Phönixgestalt?"*, 456–457.

[54] Ida Friederike Görres, " 'Engel und Teufel sind abgeschafft': Noch Vertrauen zur Kirche?" *Die Furche*, June 19, 1971, 10.

of the Novus Ordo Mass. She is aware that her audience is profoundly troubled by what is unfolding. In the lecture, she rattles off a litany of troubling manifestations of the reforms underway. She recognizes in no uncertain terms that there is a "crisis". But she does not end her lecture in dismay. Instead, her outlook extends far across time, and partway through her lecture, there is a pivot from troubling stories to making a case for trusting the Church. In the end, she responds to the crisis with the repeated affirmation "I trust in God's faithfulness."

In a letter dated April 4, 1970, to Gordan, Görres describes her preparation for this lecture:

> I recklessly agreed to give a lecture in Badenweiler on April 17: "Trusting the Church"!!!! With this, I'm getting myself into hot water!! This is like a Tunic of Nessus that does not leave one a minute's rest.[55] Today on the fourth, I have no idea what I'm going to say in thirteen days. But it is quite amusing to have to conquer, reflexively, the deepest, sustaining foundation in oneself, from which one actually lives—because I know that this is *there*, precisely because I live from it and any tribulations go only to the reflexive and conscious level, thick as swarms of hornets sometimes, but still *only* in the foreground; they never reach the foundational reason for existence—thank God. But this rather eludes expression, articulation. The desire to force oneself into this level is almost too much. At any rate, I myself am curious to see what the result will be.[56]

[55] In Greek mythology, the Tunic of Nessus was a poisoned shirt given by the centaur Nessus to Heracles, who was in agony once he put it on. The Tunic of Nessus is a metaphor for "a source of misfortune from which there is no escape". E. Cobham Brewer, "Nessus. Shirt of Nessus", *Brewer's Dictionary of Phrase and Fable*, ed. Ivor Evans, 14th ed. (New York: Harper and Row, 1989), 770.

[56] *"Wirklich die neue Phönixgestalt?"*, 456–57.

She mentions in this lecture that many fellow believers reached out to her, expressing their dismay and even fear: "People are isolated and feel abandoned in their parishes, more so than they ever did before in the unbelieving environment of their workplace. Many letters, many conversations bear witness to this. Whom should we trust?"[57]

In somewhat diplomatic terms, she wonders about the causes of "the often-strange attitude of our hierarchy" in this crisis (as in chapter 3 she wonders about "the silence of the Magisterium"). She observes, "I can imagine a widely denied but practically implemented schism, connected to Rome only by insincere verbal threads."[58] Privately during this period, she was blunter. For example, on January 30, 1970, Görres described to Gordan how she felt after seeing some of the materials circulating inside the Church in Holland. She wrote, "In view of this, I cannot understand why, in Rome, one does not simply declare schism, which has in fact long since taken place"—a schism, she said, that "is now only disguised with the contemptuous formulas of diplomacy."[59]

As she addresses this "crisis" in her lecture, her own sense of alarm is palpable. And she expects things may—or indeed will—get worse: "I can imagine the darkest development, and also I expect it."[60] Nevertheless, she balances reminders, even pleas, not to allow openness to the future to mean tossing out all Tradition with a refusal to lose hope.

Görres looks to future generations: "Maybe their grand-

[57] "Trusting the Church", p. 155.

[58] "Trusting the Church", p. 174.

[59] *"Wirklich die neue Phönixgestalt?"*, 439. See also Jennifer S. Bryson, "Why Do Heretics Remain in the Church?" *Crisis Magazine*, March 24, 2023, https://crisismagazine.com/opinion/why-do-heretics-remain-in-the-church.

[60] "Trusting the Church", p. 175.

children . . . will have had enough of trampling and rejection and will extract great discoveries from that which is defamed and withheld from them today"; and she hopes they "will receive the immortal seeds of life from the holy inheritance" and "bear them to bring forth many fruits".[61] Most importantly, she takes a long-term view, and her deep faith remains rooted in what she calls in her letter to Gordan the "foundational reason for existence"; on this foundation she affirms, "I believe in God's faithfulness."[62]

Appendix: Eulogy for Ida Friederike Görres

On May 14, 1971, Görres collapsed while delivering a passionate speech at a session of the Synod of Würzburg, at which she was a delegate. She died the next day in a hospital in Frankfurt from a cerebral hemorrhage. At the requiem Mass for her on May 19 at the Cathedral of Freiburg in Germany, Father Joseph Ratzinger, later Pope Benedict XVI, delivered the eulogy. Görres was buried in the Bergäcker Cemetery in Freiburg.

I have added Ratzinger's eulogy to this English edition of *Bread Grows in Winter* as an appendix. This eulogy is not part of the German edition of this book, which was published the year before Görres died. In this eulogy, Father Ratzinger quoted repeatedly from Görres' lecture "Trusting the Church", chapter 6 of *Bread Grows in Winter.* This is the main reason it seemed fitting to include his eulogy in this book. Also, the eulogy provides readers a way to learn more about Görres herself.

Ida Görres met Joseph Ratzinger in the late 1960s and admired him greatly. As the trends in the Church in the

[61] "Trusting the Church", p. 180.

[62] "Trusting the Church", p. 176.

1950s and especially in the 1960s evoked ever greater dismay and alarm in her, she considered him a ray of hope in a dark time. In a letter to Gordan on November 28, 1968, she called Ratzinger a "prophet in Israel". She continued, "It is *highly* encouraging that there is something like this in the new generation—and next to Küng, in Tübingen of all places! . . . May God preserve for us this champion of the old and new Church."[63] (Görres was critical of the controversial theologian Hans Küng.)[64]

Ida Görres and Joseph Ratzinger corresponded.[65] In his eulogy for her, he mentions, "In her last letter to me . . ."[66] Alfred Läpple, who had known Ratzinger since their time together in seminary in the 1940s, wrote in his book about Ratzinger that he "read books by the writer Ida Friederike Görres, who was close to him"; those books included *Bread Grows in Winter*.[67] Not only does he quote "Trusting the Church" (chapter 6 from the book) in his eulogy, but in a conversation with Peter Seewald thirty years after that eulogy, Ratzinger mentioned the title of this book when asked about the crisis in the Church. "Faith," said Ratzinger, "can lose its way if I only pray according to mood and whim. Faith also needs the discipline of the dry periods; then something grows in the silence. Just as in the winter fields, de-

[63] *"Wirklich die neue Phönixgestalt?"*, 396.

[64] Among other criticisms, Görres considered Küng "arrogant". Letter to Paulus Gordan, December 4, 1964, in *"Wirklich die neue Phönixgestalt?"*, 75.

[65] A brief segment of this correspondence was published during her lifetime: Ida Friederike Görres and Joseph Ratzinger, "Fragen eines Laien zur theologischen Diskussion über das priesterliche Amt aus einem Briefwechsel zwischen Ida Friederike Görres und Joseph Ratzinger", *Geist und Leben: Zeitschrift für Aszese und Mystik* 42, no. 3 (June 1969): 220–24.

[66] Joseph Ratzinger, "Eulogy for Ida Friederike Görres", trans. Jennifer S. Bryson, *Logos* 23, no. 4 (September 9, 2020): 148–55.

[67] Alfred Läpple, *Benedikt XVI und seine Wurzeln: Was sein Leben und seinen Glauben prägte* (Augsburg, Germany: Sankt Ulrich Verlag, 2006), 136.

spite appearances, the growth lies hidden. 'Bread grows in winter' [*sic*], is what Ida Frederike [*sic*] Görres said."[68]

Ratzinger said in his eulogy, "She spoke with an insightful certainty and a fearlessness about the pressing questions and tasks of the Church today, something which is given only to the one who truly believes."[69] He recognized that "the center of her thought and work" was "the living Church".[70] He also saw that "from this center, she was able to survive during the crisis of this mysterious organism, even to advance during the crisis and grow to a deeper understanding."[71]

The six chapters of this book bear witness to the fruitfulness in the final years of Görres' life, born out of this "center" of her life: the Church.

About This Translation

This is the first translation of *Bread Grows in Winter* into any language. Until now, there have only been the following translations of sections from it: Excerpts of "Our Image of Christ: A Letter", chapter 1, in several languages; the excerpt was included in a book that was translated several times.[72] An excerpt of "Remarks on Celibacy," chapter 5,

[68] Joseph Ratzinger, *God and the World: A Conversation with Peter Seewald*, trans. Henry Taylor (San Francisco: Ignatius Press, 2002), 321. In the German edition, the phrase translated by Taylor as "bread grows in winter," in lowercase letters, is identical to the German title of Görres' book; perhaps Taylor wrote the phrase this way because he did not recognize that this is the title of a book.

[69] "Eulogy", p. 184.

[70] "Eulogy", p. 184.

[71] "Eulogy", p. 186.

[72] Ida Friederike Görres et al., *Jesus: 2000 Jahre Glaubens- und Kulturgeschichte*

was translated into Swedish in 1971.[73] I translated "Trusting the Church: A Lecture," chapter 6, into English in 2020.[74] (For this edition, I have edited this translation lightly and expanded my annotation of it.) "Trusting the Church" was also translated into Swedish in 1971.[75]

A note about Görres' use of language is in order. She was well known not only as a Catholic but also as an author with tremendous talent and a remarkable command of the German language. Her poetry is lush and delicate. Her prose in German is often exquisite (sometimes posing special challenges for a translator). In some passages, she crafts her syntax to develop a rhythm or build momentum.

At times, she wields her pen the way a skilled fencer wields a weapon—strategically and with tactical grace and precision. One example of this the reader will see in *Bread Grows in Winter* is in the final word in five of these six chapters. In these five chapters, Görres carefully situates a poignant term as the final word to drive home a central theme of the

---

(Freiburg im Breisgau: Herder, 1999). This book was translated into Dutch, Hungarian, Polish, Russian, and Slovenian: *Jezus: 2000 jaar geloofs- en cultuurgeschiedenis* (Baarn, Netherlands: Tirion, 2000); *Jézus: 2000 éves hit-és kultúrtörténet* (Szeged, Hungary: Agapé, 2000); *Jezus: 2000 Lat Obecności* (Kraków: Wydaw, 1999); *Iisus: Dve tysjači let religii i kul'tury* (Slavija, Interbook-business, 2001); *Jezus: 2000 let zgodovine vere in kulture* (Ljubljana, Slovenia: Družina, 2002).

[73] Ida Friederike Görres, "Från Celibat till Äktenskap?", *Credo katolsk tidskrift* 51, no. 1 (1971): 9–14.

[74] Ida Friederike Görres, "Trusting the Church: A Lecture", *Logos* 23, no. 4 (Fall 2020): 123–47. An audio version of this translation was released in 2021: Ida Friederike Görres, "Trusting the Church", narrated by Karina Majewski, Catholic Culture Audiobooks, June 15, 2021, https://www.catholicculture.org/commentary/ida-friederike-grres-trusting-church/.

[75] Ida Friederike Görres, "Tillit till Kyrkan," trans. Anonymous in *Credo katolsk tidskrift* 4, no. 52 (1971): 168–74.

chapter, like a gymnast adding to the force of a great vault with a stunning, solid landing.

I first noticed this when I translated "Trusting the Church", chapter 6, in 2020. When I reached the end of this lecture, I initially translated the final sentence trying to capture the meaning of the German but focusing on the structure of the sentence on English syntax, and I thought I was done. But then I looked more closely at the German text and realized there was no way it was a coincidence that that final word of the lecture was "light" in this lecture in which Görres was trying to offer her listeners a way to navigate through a dark valley, a valley in which she was able to repeat, almost like a litany, "I believe in God's faithfulness" in spite of the darkness. I knew I had to find a way to restructure the English sentence to end the lecture in the translated version with the word "light".

Next, while translating the rest of this book a few years later, I realized that this careful placement of a key final (or penultimate) word was a pattern. In this English translation, even though I had to struggle in some of the chapters with the structure of the final sentence to maintain this, I carry this careful selection and placement of the final word over into the English text. Thus, in addition to chapter 6 ending with "light":

- "Our Image of Christ", chapter 1, exploring who Christ *is*, ends with "is", in a quote about Jesus from 1 John 3:2.
- "Demolition Troops in the Church", chapter 2, culminates forcefully with "promises to the one who repents".[76]

[76] In this case, in German, "to the one who repents" (*dem Umkehrenden*) is followed by "promises" (*zusagt*), with *zusagt* in the final position due to the rules of German sentence structure; I think Görres intended emphasis here on the relationship between the promise and the repentance, together.

- "Faith: Skeleton or Body?", chapter 3, closes with "decrease", a reference to John 3:30.
- "The Spirituality of Studying Theology", chapter 4, after Görres has emphasized that theology is not just an academic discipline but must instead be fundamentally about God and must allow space for the Holy Spirit—that is, the Flame—to work, closes emphatically with "blaze".
- "Remarks about Celibacy", chapter 5, concludes with the word "existence" (*Dasein*), underscoring that the priesthood is a state in life, an existential status, not just one of many career options.

Citations and Register of Persons

Unless otherwise noted, the citations in this English edition are my additions to the text. (The German edition of this book has only six citations.)

In just a few places, inconsistently, Görres provided a reference, such as the name of an author or a Bible verse, in parentheses in the text. Because this English edition has extensive footnotes, I have removed her original, sporadic parenthetical notes from the body of the text. I was hesitant to remove her in-text parenthetical citations because the inconsistency of them, the incomplete nature of them, and the occasional errors in them tell us something about how she worked: she appears to have been quoting from memory sometimes, and clearly she is more concerned with getting a message to her audience than providing the kind of details one would find in academic work. For ease of reading, however, I felt it was best to remove them from the text. Readers interested in this aspect of Görres' work may view the original German edition.

A few of Görres' in-text citations of Bible verses are

slightly inaccurate; I have corrected them without mentioning all the corrections in the citations. Where there was no citation for a quotation from the Bible in the German text, I have added one as a note.

For quotations from the Bible and, where possible, for quotations from other sources, I used established English translations or, in a few cases, such as quotations from Saint John Henry Newman and C. S. Lewis, the original English text. Where a quotation either has no citation (that is, when I could not find the source) or when an established translation of the source was not available, the quote is my own translation from the German. In addition, I have included a few explanatory notes.

I added a register of persons to assist English readers today who may not be familiar with some of the many people Görres mentions in her essays. There is also an index of biblical references and a general subject index. The German edition has none of these.

Orthography

When translating from German to English, the translator must make many decisions, not only in syntax and word choice but in orthography as well. In German, all nouns are capitalized. Compared with this strict rule of German, there is relatively significant flexibility in English capitalization, especially regarding religious terminology.

In capitalizing names, titles, and pronouns for God (including all members of the Trinity), as well as that which comes from God (for example, Creation, Revelation) or is exclusive to Jesus (Resurrection, Ascension, Passion), I allowed the thrust of Görres' work to serve as my guide. This book is an expression of her Catholic faith. This is so important to her that in some passages she even violates the orthography rules of German, in which all third-person pronouns are lowercase, by capitalizing "He" (Er) when referring to God. And she explains why she does this. In her "letter" in chapter 1, she writes, "Does it irritate you that I capitalize 'He'? Sorry, I don't like it any other way. The Jews, it seems to me, were quite right in not even daring to utter the name of God—and so were our ancestors, who emphasized His overwhelming otherness with at least that simple vivid allusion."

There is an exception to this capitalization, however—namely, when I quote from other sources. In these quotations, I have left the orthography as it appeared in the original text. This includes quotations from the Bible, for which I use the Revised Standard Version of the Bible: Catholic Edition, second edition (RSV-2CE), which does not capitalize pronouns referring to God.

Görres sometimes approaches language creatively and violates German's otherwise strict rules for orthography in order to emphasize a word or a point. One example of this is her tendency to separate a prefix from the rest of the word with a hyphen in order to emphasize the meaning of the prefix. Given the linguistic similarity of German and English, it has been possible to maintain this in the English translation. I put these words with the unusual hyphens in quotation marks—for example "com-municate" instead of "communicate", "re-present" instead of "represent"—to indicate that there is something special about the words, that the hyphens are not typographical errors.

The Title of This Book

Sometimes the title of a translated book differs quite significantly from the book's title in the original language. The title *Bread Grows in Winter*, however, is taken directly from the title Görres gave to this book in German, *Im Winter wächst das Brot.* Although I initially had some concerns that the phrase "Bread Grows in Winter" in English might sound odd or too vague for some readers, the meaning of this title is so central to the heart of the entire book that I felt it was imperative for the English title to reflect the German title directly.

The title *Bread Grows in Winter* echoes a reference in "Trusting the Church", chapter 6. In this lecture, after describing some of the dismay and hardship many Catholics were experiencing during the upheaval in the Church after the Second Vatican Council, even to the point of nervous breakdowns among priests, Görres wrote that this suffering "is invisible martyrs' blood. It sprouts the seeds that grow in the winter night." The image of bread in the title of this book amplifies the "seeds" mentioned in chapter 6, making the eucharistic nature of this image even more explicit.

I

Our Image of Christ: A Letter

What remains of the image of Christ we grew up with? Is it not melting away between our fingers in the torrent of new ideas that are taught to children at school, to theologians at the university, even here and there to the people from the pulpit? Was what we believe and love really just a remnant of childhood that we must resolutely cast off in order to be finally up-to-date with our era? What are we supposed to imagine as "Jesus Christ" when we can no longer rely on the Evangelists [of the Gospels]? This is what your last letter says.

And in my letter, I obviously cannot give you a sufficient answer—even if this grew into a monograph. We would have to be able to talk to each other undisturbed for days. We cannot do that. Let us just attempt this with an image—which, of course, is only shorthand, an outline of what I want to tell you. But perhaps you will understand roughly what I mean.

Imagine a mountain.[1] It does not have to be Mont Blanc;

[1] In an essay from 1956, Görres uses this same metaphor of a mountain viewed from multiple, limited perspectives to describe how we understand the Church, though she develops the metaphor slightly. Ida Friederike Görres, "Die Schatzhöhle: Ein Geleitwort", in Alfons Rosenberg *Michael und der Drache: Urgestalten von Licht und Finsternis* (Olten, Germany: Walter Verlag, 1956), 7–12. For a discussion of the image of Christ in other works

imagine any one of our beautiful hikes together that you know well.

With a thousand faces, it rests on its own in a state of repose. The forester, the painter, the geographer, the miner who travels to it—each sees it differently. It is different for the plane, which takes in the whole landscape from high in the clouds, different for the mountain farmers who live on it. The beautiful blue pyramid is always before me from my window. And the person of the petty bourgeois who, like a patient, never sees it other than through the window or from the street, perhaps thinks that this magnificent side of it is the only "correct" image and that this is what the mountain "really" looks like. He would not recognize any other picture at all. But for those who climb it, the clear triangle quickly dissolves into a tumult of disconcerting outlines; it disintegrates into foothills and uplands, into ridges, gorges, rocky slopes, valleys. And the peak one has climbed is no longer a peak at all, but a dome with a broad curve, falling steeply to the south, descending into many folds and hillocks to the north down into the valley where the road is. And consider how different every single slope looks by day and then by night—in the morning fog, in the moonlight—and how different just with the changing of the seasons!

Inexhaustible variations. A thousand snapshots, a hundred sketches—do they contradict each other? Who could call one wrong, the other right? The spiritual "points of view" vary almost like those of the senses. The land surveyor translates his "rendering" into dots and dashes—

---

by Görres, see Michael Kleinert, *Es wächst viel Brot in der Winternacht: Theologische Grundlinien im Werk von Ida Friederike Görres* (Würzburg: Echter, 2002), 90–93.

incomprehensible scribbles for the farmer's wife on the farmstead; she is shaped by the mountain right down to her physique and facial features, and she knows its vagaries and weather better than all the academic geographers down in the valley. The geologist strips the mountain of its immense furlike outer layers of forest, meadows, settlements, and roads and "sees" only the ancient rock core, on which he "reads" ice ages, outbreaks of fire, and geological layers. The hiker experiences it with body and soul and stores memories of colors, scents, frights, exertion, and incomparable rest. And so forth. Who can play the "views" off against each other? They all describe the same reality, which no individual can grasp, which all complement each other, and, from this, the big picture is established: *the mountain*. But the mountain and its best, most comprehensive picture are still two different things. It is similar for us with our image of Christ.

~

Theology, dogmatics—these are maps, if you will. Lots of curious ciphers, an extreme concentration of endless intellectual work, the essences from many contradictions, the work of specialists in formulas of a special jargon: God's Only Begotten Son, the Second Divine Person, God-Man, Two Natures in One Person, and so on.

The Evangelists tell of diapers and tears, of sleep and hunger, of anger and fear; "how the Lord has been so gentle, without guile and without deceit";[2] of the Herald and

[2] This is from a poem by the German Protestant poet Luise Hensel: "Jesus in der Heiligen Schrift", in Winfried Freund, *Müde bin ich, geh' zur Ruh: Leben und Werk der Luise Hensel* (Wiedenbrück, Germany: Güth + Etscheidt, 1984), 81.

the Miracle-Worker, of the One who was betrayed and executed; "My God, my God, why have you forsaken me?"[3] and of an open grave and Resurrection. But already the letters of the Apostles say succinctly and powerfully: "This is the true God and eternal life" (1 John 5:20). (People really ought to read the Epistles a lot more; who among us really knows them?) And "He reflects the glory of God and bears the very stamp of his nature, upholding the universe by his word of power" (Heb 1:3). "He is the image of the invisible God, the first-born of all creation; . . . all things were created through him and for him" (Col 1:15–16).

~

And then the Apocalypse with its surrealistic images: the Son of Man with stars and lampstands, a sword coming out of His mouth; the seven-eyed, seven-horned Lamb; the many-crowned Rider on the white horse.[4]

The liturgy presents itself to us as the place and manner of His present ministry: He baptizes, He bestows His Spirit, He absolves us of our sins. The priest, as His instrument, shows us the Host: "Behold the Lamb of God!"; and we address the Host as a person: "Lord, I am not worthy"! And the Church proclaims herself His Body, His people, His bride, His city, His placeholder until He comes again.

(Does it irritate you that I capitalize "He"? Sorry, I don't like it any other way. The Jews, it seems to me, were quite right in not even daring to utter the name of God—and so were our ancestors, who emphasized His overwhelming otherness with at least that simple vivid allusion.)

The older exegesis endlessly brooded over every word of

[3] Ps 22:1; Mt 27:46.

[4] See Rev 1:12–20; 19:11–15; 5:6; 6:2.

Holy Scripture and examined and interpreted it with a double or triple meaning—literal, moral, mystical; certainly, also imprecise, also fanciful and artificial. Still, it was important enough for them to care. They found traces of Him throughout the Old Testament—types, symbols, promises, all fulfilled in Him—it is all smelted down wonderfully in our liturgy.

And just the testimony of the saints, the mystics: about the most personal, solitary experience, about bodily encounter, in images and in that which has no image. They dare to apply the entire Song of Songs in their testimony without being ashamed or afraid—sometimes it is the voice of the Church, sometimes of a believing soul. Some visibly bear His stigmata, others heal and save in His name; all possess a radiant, often overwhelming resemblance to Him, recognizable even to hardened and distant minds.

And so, today, comes the most recent exegesis from the outside penetrating into the Church and, as you say, it is eagerly taken up—and thus it claims that Christ is merely a faceless, shadowy outline from twenty centuries ago; nothing is known for certain, not even whether He really lived; nothing can be proven strictly historically. (It is not so recent, by the way. Among our neighbors using the other prayer book, it is already about a hundred years old; it is only among us that it is a *dernier cri*—that is, the latest fashion!) No detail of the Tradition is irrefutably certain; we can only grasp the echo of His effect on His disciples, their "Christ experience", which is a psychological process. And even this is not pure and reliable in our investigation but, rather, is hardly recognizable anymore, thickly painted over, in fragments, overgrown with various alienating encrustations of language and also unforeseeably changed by later anonymous insertions, by pedagogical intentions, by time-bound mythical templates for thought, through legends retold in various ways and recollections inserted retrospectively into the Old Testament.

Why are you so upset about this? *That* should actually be the central question. You neither know the professors involved, nor do you read their books; you really know their intentions only from the echo of hearsay, from rumors about sermons, from panel discussions on television, from articles in popular magazines at Christmas, and, last but not least, from our Church media, which have become so brash and whose standards you have not really viewed as particularly honorable so far. So why does this—precisely this dubious mishmash—rattle you so much that you have to fear that the image of Christ that we have inherited will ultimately be discredited by it once and for all? This psychological curiosity would actually be the "thorny problem"; why do you—and so many, many Catholics—believe this vague something-or-other more willingly than the entirety of the Church, including the Magisterium?

That question, of course, deserves a separate letter. Let us stay with your question and my image for today. So, people who have never been on a mountain show up and explain to you that, first of all, it is an open question whether there are such things as "mountains" or whether this idea is not a naive, fanciful attempt to explain certain cloud formations on the horizon. Others say, as far as your special mountain is concerned, that only the following is certain about it: First, that its name is an incomprehensible relic from a lost, indeterminate tribal language; despite some echoes of, let us say, Celtic dialects, philology still cannot say exactly what those syllables might have meant at the supposed time of that extinct people. Furthermore, it is certain that this designation on the map is used today for a miniscule shade-dwelling snail. But one would first have to do academic research into: when the word and symbol first appeared on a map; since when have there been maps at all; what types of maps were used in antiquity, the Middle Ages, and modern times, and on what basis—empirical or fanciful, mythological or legendary, or based on travelogues; furthermore, one would have to know the authorities and methods of their transmission and who commissioned and produced them; furthermore, the conventions of their map legends, the changing interpretation and meaning of the graphic signs, their references to astronomical and astrological ciphers, the folklore associated with them in various epochs and lands, and much more. Those who are interested can glean enormous amounts of information about cartography from this. But of what use is it to those who want to find out more about this particular mountain in order to climb it? Despite or because of the most extensive avoidance of all conceivable adjacent areas, the only thing proven—really convincingly—is that one has almost nothing to say about *the topic itself.*

Something that really cannot be said of our "inherited" image of Christ.

But—why, actually, do you absolutely want to "imagine" it?

No one can simply "imagine" the totality of Church statements about Jesus the Christ, any more than the totality of physical and astronomical facts. People have "always known" that. The Trinity, for example, can be made graphic only in symbols—here too, in ciphers and formulas.

Once again, I have to quote old Möhler; the way he puts it is unsurpassable: "Only in the whole can he who created the whole be known because he reveals himself completely only in the whole. How is the single individual to know him? Only because the individual, although not the whole, can yet embrace it with great mind, with love. Thus, although the individual is not the whole, the whole is yet in the individual and the individual knows what the whole is."[5]

This whole is the Church, and her alone.

You know, when I say "Church", I never mean just the Catholics, which is what is buzzing around under that name these days; no thanks, belonging only to the "club"—I don't know if it would be worth the trouble for me![6] "Church", for me, is always and necessarily the great entity, the mysterious living being, rooted in the days of the Apostles and which will experience the Day of Judgment; the only one, the ancient contemporary of the Lord and His first disci-

[5] Johann Adam Möhler, *Unity in the Church, or, The Principle of Catholicism: Presented in the Spirit of the Church Fathers of the First Three Centuries*, trans. Peter C. Erb (Washington, D.C.: Catholic University of America Press, 2016), 153.

[6] I think that what Görres means here by "I never mean just the Catholics" should not be understood as an affirmation of the increasingly vague ecumenical movement at the time this essay was written in 1968. Instead, I believe this statement reflects her rejection of "what is buzzing around under that name" of Catholic "these days"—namely, the narrow, clublike "Team Catholic!" understanding of the Church. In a 1960 essay about what it means to "belong" to the Church, she explained her uneasiness with this type of belonging. She writes, "Others belong to the Church as to a 'religious party', as the Baroque period quite bluntly called 'confessions'. They are the patriots of their 'religious party'; they have devoted themselves to the good cause and now feel bound by a sense of honor and self-respect to persevere there, come what may and unwaveringly, whatever it may cost." Ida Friederike Görres, "Laie und Kirche," *Der Christliche Sonntag* (June 19, 1960), 197–98. (This essay has been translated into English by Jennifer S. Bryson and will appear in a forthcoming anthology of essays by Görres on the Church.) Also, later in this chapter, she alludes to her uneasiness with the sense among some that being Catholic means merely being part of a "club": "Christians are, in general, a ridiculous minority around the globe . . . ; and the "real Christians" have always been so in the midst of the 'club members'." (P. 68.)

ples, who, since then, has been living uninterruptedly with the Living and Exalted One, as in a marriage, according to the Letter to the Corinthians.[7] She really knows Whom she is talking about, and that is why one should listen to her. This is why no one can persuade her that her Companion for life—Christ "yesterday and today and for ever"![8]—is an undefined shadow of dead brains; that is, of the brains of dead men. In her memory and consciousness, the thousand partial views, memories, experiences, and interpretations melt together into an immense mysterious figure, a countenance that we mean when we say "Christ". Two thousand years have worked on this picture, a huge mosaic—countless nameless people, and some well-known and famous ones, have compiled and formed it. But at the same time, it is a living image, one that has developed, arising from a double, simultaneous process: from the tremendous, loyal human effort, persevered in from generation to generation *and* from the slow, free, deliberate self-disclosure of the Lord, as one friend "com-municates" himself more and more to a friend through the years, always letting him be more deeply in the know, entrusting himself to him more and more openly.

It is not exactly startling news that Jesus' image in the Gospels is mysterious and difficult to interpret, is it? Only the *results* of these efforts are so familiar to us that we take them "for granted", the way every child takes the achievements of technology for granted. Already, "back then" is emphasized; how little His environment understood Him during His lifetime. Only in retrospect, from the experience of Easter, from the illumination of Pentecost, did even

[7] See 2 Cor 11:2; 1 Cor 7.

[8] Heb 13:8.

the Apostles learn to comprehend their experiences, to express them through meaning and context. The Lord had expressly promised them that the Holy Spirit—and only He!—would lead them to understand what He had told them. Yes, I know, here you will say, "And what if the farewell speeches are not 'real' but only 'edited' by John or someone else?"

I do not mind. For certain, we have considered the New Testament too much as a whole until now (though not out of sheer stupidity, as you fear, rather out of quite respectable motives). We are happy to let ourselves be guided by *faithful* exegesis—because that does the job too, not just the fundamentally unbelieving sort!—to be taught that the structure of the Gospels is much more complicated than we previously knew. And we knew that they are not simply narratives "in a single unit" but, rather, are artfully (or accidentally, or improvisatorially—that is irrelevant) assembled collections of sayings and clusters of parables with memories of experiences inserted as bridges. And if, here and there, when copies were made, mistakes have been made, ones that change meaning, or a later wording has replaced an original one, or a copyist might even have inserted a sentence of his own reflection: Does it bother you, would it bother you, if someone could prove to you with a microscope and chemistry that in the bread and wine of our Mass, sterile grains are also ground, rotten grapes also get pressed?

The miracle of Christ's Presence is not due to its material quality. Very similarly, it seems to me (C. S. Lewis alludes to this in a letter[9]), the Church has taken the New Testament Scriptures into her hands *as they are*, with their inconsisten-

[9] Görres is most likely referring to C. S. Lewis, "Modern Theology and Biblical Criticism", in *Christian Reflections*, ed. Walter Hooper (Grand Rapids: William B. Eerdmans, 1967), 152–66. She translated this essay into German: C. S. Lewis, "Moderne Theologie und Bibelkritik: Ein Vortrag", *Erbe und*

cies and minor errors—and, *by* accepting them, has "consecrated" them to the Word of God. Understand this: it is just as conceivable and probable as it is unprovable that the Evangelists, for example, did not reproduce many of the Lord's speeches verbatim but, rather, abbreviated them in their own words, but true to the meaning, the way we also report on what we have heard. Other sentences that He spoke may, in turn, have been burned into their hearts, indelibly, such that they would not have moved one letter out of place. But who is going to pick this apart? No exegesis can do that. Jesus Christ is the Lord of the Church, alive and working in her. This means that, where it has been accepted and confirmed, *there He Himself, in the same act,* MAKES *that transformation of His Word "back then" into His "present" speech to us.* That, too, is a kind of transformation of what is. As it stands now, it is His Word, and we believe it confidently.

Throughout the existence of the Church, understanding continues to grow, even though again and again it is cast into shadow and covered over by the sins of believers. The Reality of the Lord is so inexhaustible that no individual, no group, no generation by themselves can comprehend and express it. That we are historical beings is, especially today, the most popular assertion—when it is to be proved to us that the past is no longer valid for us. But that we are historical beings also means that we must preserve and assimilate what came before, because we can discern and act only in succession. What is it like for us, as persons? It is true that there is

---

Auftrag 44, no. 4 (1968): 291–302. It is not clear, however, why she says here that this was "in a letter". Alternatively, though I think less likely, Görres may be referring to C. S. Lewis, letter to Arthur Greeves, December 6, 1931, in *The Collected Letters of C. S. Lewis*, vol. 2, ed. Walter Hooper (San Francisco: HarperSanFrancisco, 2004), 22–23.

the flash of intuition, the well-known love at first sight (*coup de foudre*), that reveals one to the other "in an instant". But it is quite rare, and, even then, the single flash must gradually clarify and confirm itself. How long is the route from the first moment of falling in love, from the first conversation, through a long marriage or friendship! How much still remains mysterious to us about the other person—indeed, does not the growing knowledge beget ever-new enigmas?

~

To develop: that means that something is already enclosed, as in a wrapper, but is still imperceptible. You must have often watched when a poppy flower burst its bud and the tiny, shapeless crumpled thing literally "un-folded" into wonderfully wide, smooth petals. The early Church was, in many respects, a bud, harboring infinite yield. But only the fully grown tree shows "what really came out of it", that is, what "was actually in it".[10]

This tree, which gradually grew out of it through many transformations—this is the image of Christ that the Church "put[s] forward . . . to be received by faith".[11] This will not be understood there, where one would like to pull us back before the whole development and again pin it down to the dry apple seed that some theologians think they will be able to carve out, like a dissection, as the "faith of the Apos-

[10] Görres develops the image of the Church as "tree"—and "bedrock" as well—in depth in chapter 2, "Bedrock and Tree", of *The Church in the Flesh*. Ida Friederike Görres, *The Church in the Flesh*, trans. Jennifer S. Bryson (Providence: Cluny Media, 2023), 30–52.

[11] Rom 3:25.

tles". That does not seem any more sensible to me than if someone were to suggest that we do away with all lighting and heating technology and make do with whatever fire we can get out of rubbing sticks together and striking stones.

The faith of the Apostles was only a beginning. Everything was in it but still undeveloped. Even the earliest "snapshots" in the memory of the disciples, which we find in the Gospels, were just like exposed film, which has to be tended—"brooded over"—in chemical solutions, following an indispensable series of steps in the darkroom, until the next "carrier" can show the full print; in the depths of the Church's consciousness, those early memories gradually emerged and were "fixed" [that is, imprinted].[12] We live from the result—when we "embrace the whole thing with great heart, with love".[13] If not, the parts disintegrate; they fall away on their own without the living bond.

[12] In predigital photography, a "latent image" is first captured on a light-sensitive surface, such as film, when it is exposed to light. This is what Görres means by "exposed film". Next comes a crucial, difficult step: the film with the latent image must be developed in a darkroom in special chemicals to "draw out" the image. The film is placed in a film-developer fluid, and the timing of this step must be controlled with precision. The careful, constant attention that this process requires is what Görres analogously calls "brooding", the way a hen broods over her eggs. If the film with the latent image is developed properly, it can then be duplicated numberless times on photographic paper when a device using light casts the latent image from the properly developed film onto a "carrier", such as photographic paper. The carrier is then submerged in a chemical solution, a process called "fixing", which solidifies an imprint of the initial latent image on the carrier. For Görres, the memories of the disciples are like exposed film that needed to be developed with care, and then this memory was later "fixed" in the depth of the consciousness of the Church. (Special thanks to photographer Michael Hansmann for helping me understand this process.)

[13] See Mark 13:33.

That process of development can partially be viewed by backtracking, but it cannot be rewound. It is irreversible and irrevocable. But it is also not yet over.

~

I find it breathtaking to look at even the roughest outlines of it. Remember: when we go on a hike, the sights of the mountain lying in repose change for us as we go along. The whole history of the Church bears witness to such a trek of Christianity—from one twisting-and-turning to another. In the panorama of the Church year, the liturgy transforms its image of Christ, and ever-new feasts (some well and some less-well devised and made!) set the accents. Piety lingers in the ascent through the centuries again and again on a different point—technically this is called "a devotion": to the Risen One, to the Man of Sorrows, to the Heart of Jesus. This sequence of motifs can be clearly traced in Christian art.

The martyrs—from Stephen onward!—"see" the Exalted Lord, as icons still prefer to do. From the Victor of Easter, He "unfolds" into the Universal Ruler, to the Heavenly Emperor, to the Crown Bearer—all variations of the aspect of Him being the "one seated on the throne".[14] From this perspective, I must say that the virtuous indignation at "triumphalism", an indignation that is now in fashion among Catholics, often strikes me as rather absurd. For me, this aspect, now thoroughly condemned, has its main root in the intensive experience of precisely this genuine and legitimate declaration: Divine Majesty, "the ruler of kings on

[14] Rev 4:2. Regarding Christ as the "Crown Bearer", see also chapter 5, "The Enthroned", in Görres, *The Church in the Flesh*, 148–82.

earth''[15]—and this is despite all the historical degradations of this. Many popes and bishops have felt themselves to be His representatives and envoys, more of the Christ who is *present* than of the historical Jesus of Nazareth—and they were right about this, even if they often drew rather inappropriate consequences for their own benefit. And before envy became the all-pervasive sociological world power it is today, believers, without envy and resentment, grasped this, recognized it, honored it, rejoiced, and were proud of it!

This is an aside. But the stars are also on the move—not just us!—and another star rose: the head full of blood and wounds, the Crucified One, the Lord God suffering and on the lap of the Pietà.

For me, this process results in an X-ray image of the mysterious, inner history of the Church, which, each time, discovers and reflects a new feature in the face of Christ and seeks to embody it. Think of Bernard and Francis and Catherine of Siena! Ignatius then "sees" the Divine Majesty again—as the Spaniards in general do—but with a new accent: the "Commander in Chief", the two banners.[16] In addition, the Baroque-era crowned God-child figures, such as the Infant Jesus of Prague, are a strange variation of the same motif: the Little King of Grace (*Petit Roi de la Gloire*) in the figure of one who has fainted. Entire orders arise from such changing impulses—each of the major foundations reflects a special guise of Christ: Benedictines, Franciscans, Jesuits;

[15] Rev 1:5.

[16] Ignatius of Loyola, *The Spiritual Exercises of St. Ignatius of Loyola*, trans. Elder Mullan (New York: P. J. Kenedy and Sons, 1914), 73, https://archive.org/details/spiritualexercis00ignauoft. Regarding "the two banners", or standards, in his "Meditation on Two Standards", Ignatius writes about "how Christ calls and wants all under His standard; and Lucifer, on the contrary, under his" (73).

even more "special" are the later, smaller foundations: Passionists, Sacramentinos, congregations of the Sacred Heart, of the Precious Blood.[17] Last but not least, the whole devotion to Mary! For when looked at more closely, it is nothing other than a fruit and consequence of the understanding of Christ—right down to its most peculiar excesses, which mostly reflect the degradation in the understanding of Christ in a strangely complementary way.

For example, we have witnessed a major turning point, and we are still standing in the curve: in the modern example of the great pendulum swing, which is playing out in the consciousness of faith between the two christological poles of God and man. Forgotten heresies embody this tension even in the early days of the Church. But what does "forgotten" mean? Only the names change; the errors are rooted in our innate one-sidedness. If the mind concentrates on the statement "God", the other half easily blurs to the point of unreality. One attributes to Christ only a pseudobody, a pseudobirth, a pseudodeath. The apocryphal gospels weren't the only things to grow out of such a mentality. The nineteenth century, up to the First World War, also lived amid the same "docetic" misconception that deeply saturated not only popular devotional literature and artistic kitsch, but also the theology of sermons, devotions, and retreats.

In the "Savior" with whom we grew up, was not the man Jesus completely dissolved into His Divinity? What remained of Him but the highly abstract formula: "His most Holy Humanity"? In paintings and little pictures, we see the

[17] That is, Congregatio Passionis Iesu Christi (CP) and Congregatio Sanctissimi Sacramenti (SSS). There are many religious orders with "Sacred Heart" and "Precious Blood" in their names.

Holy Family being served by angels, the boy thoughtfully assembling small pieces of wood; later, as a youth, He puts together beams to form a cross; Our Lady, at the manger, with heavy tears on her cheeks, while the vision of the three crosses rises threateningly before her (an image as chilling as it is popular!). The adolescent in Nazareth was like a young musical genius who must not touch a piano, concealing His full power for miracles at every moment in painful obedience. The wandering, preaching Lord had His omniscience, His omnipotence fully conscious and available all the time; His questions are only pro forma, as His temptations in the desert are only a spectacle; even His prayer in Gethsemane is still pedagogical, as though a model for us. "Isn't it true, now He is only God again?" asked a girl after a sermon on the Ascension. In essence, this is the Indian concept of the avatar, the descending deity who puts on and takes off a human body "like a glove", as in Goethe's "Bayadere".[18] Karl Rahner's very important essay "The Eternal Significance of Jesus's Humanity for Our Relationship with God", in the third volume of his *Theological Writings*, proves that related attitudes, in a more complicated rather than naive tone, are still present.[19]

Then came the turnaround: the flood of "Life of Jesus" publications, the novels about Christ, from the late nineteenth century to the 1920s, even up to Dorothy Sayers' radio drama, *The Man Born to Be King*, still during the

[18] Johann Wolfgang von Goethe, "The God and the Bayadere", in *Goethe*, trans. John Whaley (London: Everyman, 2000), 48–50.

[19] Karl Rahner, "Die ewige Bedeutung der Menschheit Jesu für unser Gottesverhältnis", in *Menschsein und Menschwerdung Gottes: Studien zur Grundlegung der Dogmatik, zur Christologie, Theologischen Anthropologie und Eschatologie*, ed. H. Vorgrimler, Sämtliche Werke (Freiburg im Breisgau: Herder, 2005), vol. 12, 251–60.

last war.[20] Fortunately, they have been forgotten—oh, how kitschy most of them were; what a juicy roast they would be to today's critics, as full of blunders in theology as they are in terms of cultural history! Nevertheless: a single touching testimony for the glowing desire of Christianity, feeling its way, to present Jesus to the people once again! I think back on these shabby creations, with grateful affection, if also with wistful amusement. They helped me a great deal to break out of the "paradigm prison" of sermons and religion class; *Ben Hur*, for example—as little as I liked his strangely feminine, ailing Christ even back then—but the era and environment did come alive.[21] I also gratefully remember a really dreadful kitsch novel, *Jesus the Young Man*, by a Protestant, ultraliberal ex-pastor: tasteless to the point of silliness, but like a cold shock it made me aware of our quasi-docetic caricature of the Jesus who is only heavenly.[22] The once very popular "realistic" paintings by Gebhard Fugel about the Bible provided the same service for us; they "translated" the antique or classic stage characters in costumes, with curly coifs, such as in the work of Thorvaldsen, into gaunt Bedouins with headscarves and burnous, aside campfires and wandering through geographically "realistic" landscapes; how startling real the "biblical stories" became, snatched from the late-"Nazarene" layer of gloss![23] Later, I recognized the Lord, again and again, in

[20] Dorothy Sayers, *The Man Born to Be King. A Play-Cycle on the Life of Our Lord Jesus Christ* (London: Victor Gollancz, 1943).

[21] Görres appears to be referring either to *Ben-Hur: A Tale of the Christ*, directed by Fred Niblo (Metro-Goldwyn-Mayer, 1925) or *Ben Hur*, directed by William Wyler (Metro-Goldwyn-Mayer, 1959).

[22] Wilhelm Scharrelmann, *Jesus der Jüngling* (Leipzig, Germany: Quelle and Meyer, 1925).

[23] Görres is probably referring to the 136 paintings of scenes of the Bible

Martin Buber's Eastern Jewish tzaddikim (righteous ones) with their disciples—for example, in the "holy Jew" Jaakow Jizchak ben Ascher of Przysucha.[24] That is how it may have been! And in Sholem Asch's novel from the same milieu, *Mottke the Vagabond*, and in Werfel's novel about Jeremiah, in which, behind the figure of the prophet, the Lord, unnamed, constantly, reverently shines through with startling clarity.[25] I think I recognize him more in these Jewish mirrors than in our mostly so unspeakably tame, late-European, late-civilization fantasy figures.

Today, this trend has already reached its extreme. Even believing theologians emphasize only the "Simple Man"; they hardly dare to grant something miraculous to His life anymore, and therefore they are annoyed by the virgin conception and birth. The "God-Side" ("GottSeite" [*sic*])

---

by Fugel from 1908–1932, collected in Gebhard Fugel, *Biblische Schulwandbilder* (Munich: Ars Sacra, J. Mueller, 1931–1939). "Nazarene" refers to the artistic movement within nineteenth-century German Romanticism to reintroduce spiritual, including biblical, themes into art.

[24] Jaakow Jizchak ben Ascher (1766–1813) was a Hasidic rabbi in Przysucha, Poland.

[25] The title of the novel by Sholem (also known as Schalom and Sholom) Asch (and Ash) Görres mentions is *Der Sackträger*. *Sackträger* means vagabond. However, she is likely referring to this novel: Sholom Ash, *Mottke the Vagabond (Mottke Ganef)*, trans. Isaac Goldberg (Boston: John W. Luce and Company, 1917). Ash, *Mottke the Vagabond*, v. The original Yiddish title of this novel is *Moṭḳe Ganev*. (*Moṭḳe* is short for Mordechai and *Ganev* means thief.) The German translation is Schalom Asch, *Mottke der Dieb*, trans. Georg Richter (Berlin: I. Ladyschnikow Verlag, 1926); this title translates as "Mottke the Thief". (Goldberg notes that the word he translates into English as "vagabond" could also be translated as "thief" or "scamp".) I found no translation of *Moṭḳe Ganev* titled *Der Sackträger*. Perhaps Görres was referring to the title by memory and recalled the gist of the story but not the exact title. The novel by Franz Werfel is *Hearken unto the Voice*, trans. Moray Firth (London: Jarrolds, 1938), first published in German in 1837.

suffocates in the flesh; the dogmatic tradition is simply switched off. This is certainly an important root of the fight against our devotion to Mary. Mary is felt to be a real nuisance because she so clearly testifies to that other side. That which must not be, cannot be. In this theology that no longer has belief, Rabbi Yeshua dissolves into a faceless echo.

~

But the Church, the pilgrim Church, sees Him anew in form and countenance at this bend in the road. As usual, it is saints and seers—not theology departments!—who, as on a high mountain, are the first to feel the rays of a sunrise.

Today, we are witnessing quite clearly how Charles de Foucauld and Teilhard de Chardin powerfully call hitherto unknown or "silent" aspects of His reality into the consciousness of the Church: what opposite poles, and yet both convincing, and how fruitful!

Foucauld saw and proclaimed the hidden, the inconspicuous Jesus of Nazareth, the Christ "in the last place",[26] as it were, "Jesus the layman", before He takes up His office as prophet and sacrifice. Teilhard saw the cosmic Christ, as He was already mysteriously indicated in some Pauline letters: the ultimate meaning of the world, the origin of all Creation, its path and Omega point, Christ clothed with the universe, transforming it into a single [eucharistic] Host. We already see a whole throng of disciples, shaped by Foucauld's teaching, permeating the Church like a catalyst. Teil-

[26] "In the last place" is a phrase from the outline for the rule of the "Little Brothers of Jesus" by Charles de Foucauld in 1896 and from "Meditations". See Jean-François Six, *Witness in the Desert: The Life of Charles de Foucauld*, trans. Lucie Noel (New York: Macmillan, 1965), 51–53, 264, 266.

hard's thought seems at first to be a plaything of intellectuals; perhaps we will also experience surprising formations of community from it.

It seems childish to me to play off the facets of this richness polemically against each other. The figure of the Infant Jesus, although it—as a figure—can also be more easily corrupted, does not become kitschy just because there is also the Man of Sorrows; just as little as the Crucified and the Risen do not refute or cancel each other out. At the moment, contempt for Nativity scenes is in fashion, scenes that for generations reproduced our account of Saint Luke in simple period costumes. Granting all the excesses, the content itself is not "false Romanticism", as its opponents claim; theirs is probably the naive idea that diapers and stable dung are idyllic and poetic things—the critics have probably never had to touch either of them.

No, every partial view can be right as long as it remains within the whole in the proportion it deserves, and each partial view that is pulled out and isolated can be wrong. The medieval isolation of [Jesus as] the "Strict Judge of All Sins" necessarily had to exaggerate Mary as the intercessor, as the only figure of mercy in the face of an eternally angry, punishing God. It is like the way today that those singling out Jesus' combative speeches against the Pharisees want to reduce Him to an "angry young man". In our boarding-school education, we still saw the pale and feeble defective result of the great mysticism of the Passion and the great bridal mysticism quite severely: "Bridegroom of the Soul", weeping, begging for comfort, the "Prisoner in the Tabernacle" whom one has to keep company, so to speak.

As a raised hand can cover the whole landscape, so such an aspect torn out can cover the whole figure of the Lord.

But even within a distorted perspective, both the hand and the landscape remain facts.

~

Yet, this whole time we are still talking only about the IMAGE. In reality, this is about Him, the Person Himself, who is "put forward . . . to be received by faith"[27] in all His images.

And this, you see, distinguishes our relationship with Christ essentially, absolutely, from that of all those who merely "concern themselves" with Him as an object of many academic and semiacademic disciplines. They talk *about* Him; we talk *to* Him. That is a huge difference. They think that research must first find out who He was in the first place, what He actually said, and what He actually meant by that which has been established with great difficulty.

For us, He is Someone who dwells in our midst and with whom we interact daily. I do not even mean first or even exclusively His eucharistic Presence, in Mass and the Supper and in the mysterious "tent" of His sojourn that we still call a "tabernacle", as the ancient Jews called the place in the desert that God's Glory sometimes suffused; the tabernacle around which the love and joy of our ancestors built the most beautiful houses, really as houses of God and not just as meeting places for congregations. No, I mean Him as the tremendously active principle of life for our Church, acting, vigorously interfering in our destiny. "To imagine": for decades I have not been able to form an "inner picture of Him"; most of the obvious images are unbearable to me; their impropriety surges into my consciousness as if

[27] Rom 3:25.

it were screeching. But know this: I see Him calling people all around, calling them, laying hands on them, and just seizing them for Himself—exactly, really exactly as it says in the Gospel, "called to him those whom he desired".[28] And people are then bound, hand and foot, as firmly as in a marriage, there for nothing else but for Him. There are millions; you know this, your brother is also among them. And there are millions of others—not as publicly recognizable as with "those who are consecrated"[29], who are the "sign" for us all, but for them, too, He is the center of their existence; they measure everything they do and do not do by His Word and Will, by its effect for His Kingdom. And still others are not "pious" at all, but when it comes down to it, His Commandments and prohibitions are the final guideline of their decisions; they submit to the Church just because they believe she represents His Will; thus, angrily and gnashing their teeth, they submit. Yet I think of the unhappy ones who do not divorce because of this, of the divorced who forgo a second marriage to someone newly discovered—staggering testimonies that He is Lord!

And others, countless others, live quite happily without Him, but they cannot die without being reconciled to Him. And think of all the peoples and countries where being a Christian means renouncing everything that people otherwise seek and appreciate as fulfillment in life! I heard, from a very reliable source, about a highly talented young man in the Eastern Bloc who was offered a fast track and an attractive career by a Party official if he would join them. At last, the official said angrily, since the other man was still

[28] Mk 3:13.
[29] See Num 6.

silent, "What else do you want that we cannot give you?" "Christ", said the young man. "And I cannot live without Him."

Are not these also experience-based facts, no less real than the geographical, geological facts of our "mountain"? Can you explain them away as smoke and mirrors?

We know "a lot" about Him; we know "little"—both are true. But at least we know enough to live with Him, to be able to talk to Him.

And life is more important than all the theories about it. People ate before they talked about vitamins and calories; people had children before the most learned doctors had any notion about hormones and genes. And if professors were arguing today about the "correct" composition of air, we could not hold our breath until one party could publish its victory from a laboratory.

People lived with Christ before the Gospels were written. People today must and can live with Him, for Him, behind iron and bamboo curtains,[30] without professors and universities, without books and lectures, even without Mass—and, as one hears, they can do it even much better than we can. The reports are stunning and shameful.

Tell me: Why are we so ashamed of the fact that we are offered more of the message and understanding of Christ through and in the Church than "those outside"? At least offered, even if we unfortunately take in far too little of it

[30] During the Cold War, the Iron Curtain was the line of demarcation between the communist states and noncommunist states, especially in Europe. The Bamboo Curtain was the line of demarcation between the communist states in Asia, especially China, and the noncommunist states.

and do even less with it? But we are embarrassed to acknowledge it and so we deny it, belittle it, criticize it, ignore it.

This is very often the reason for our strange seesaw posture. Of course, it is only part of a powerful psychological wave sweeping the world today: the turmoil of being conscious of ownership, the shame of the haves before the have-nots. This creates the urge to hide what is one's own, to cover up the differences as much as possible. Part of it is fear, an assiduous evasion, camouflaging oneself from the global power of envy. In part, it is the noble urge "not to have it better than others"—even then, not always without the timid dread of the odium of the principle *beati possidentes* (blessed are those who possess). This magnanimous urge to put oneself on an equal footing with the poor, with the lowly, works among the disciples of Foucauld as well as in the worker priests. But that makes sense only if my divestment really benefits others. What cripple would benefit if ten healthy people got crutches and seemed to be limping? Which blind person would be helped by others' gluing their eyes shut?

In the spiritual realm, it is no different. What we have is given to us to share: this is a most basic law. We cannot "help it" if "receiving that we may give" is destined for us, and, for this very reason, we should not do anything about it, out of a squeamishness that would be not noble but cowardly. We have also been told with outright emphasis: "But blessed are your eyes, for they see, and your ears, for they hear. Truly, I say to you, many prophets and righteous men longed to see what you see, and did not see it, and to hear what you hear, and did not hear it."[31] There it is, written quite bluntly: that our merit—for it is such!—has nothing

[31] Mt 13:16–17.

to do with "worthiness". "Prophets and righteous men"! Yes, by human standards, we would have to hide from them, but we have received something that is denied to them—out of that divine "injustice" that so frightens us and that the Lord is so fond of emphasizing in the parables. Here, too, we can only obey, accept, take up, and pass it on as intact as possible. At least testify that it exists.

~

One more thing—you ask at the end of your letter: "Aren't we, who still hold on to the 'full' Catholic faith, gradually becoming a ridiculous minority after all?"

I cannot judge this. In the rising waves of confusion in which we live today, with "expression of opinion" so unequal, so cleverly manipulated, and the exploitation of opinion by the people who make "public opinion", even in the Church, the actual proportions are simply incalculable. Sometimes, from distant memory, the sentence comes forcefully to mind: "Faith makes mute, unbelief eloquent." For many who do not explicitly possess the gift of being articulate, this may be true.

Christians are, in general, a ridiculous minority around the globe, already according to their external standing; and the "real Christians" have always been so in the midst of the "club members". We who live today are, in turn, such a minority, in the view of the countless generations that have passed away—we are the foliage of one summer on an ancient tree. And if, within all these concentric circles, "we" are still one of them, what does this mean?

The Lord of the Church still meets us in His Church—still! We do not know how much longer we will still experience the freedom to preach. We are still able to explore

Him as a landscape, consume Him as food, sink our roots into Him as a plant does into the ground. Nevertheless—I repeat it ad nauseum—nevertheless, everything that the Church "puts forward"[32] to us of Him reveals and conceals Him at the same time, "betrays" Him in the double sense of the word. Everything. But it is still there, abundantly on offer, never exhausted in our whole life. Let us joyfully, gratefully accept as much as our eyes and hearts can take in and bear. One day He, the Near and the Far, the Familiar and the Incomprehensible, the Unimaginable, will meet us behind the threshold—"as he" really "is."[33]

[32] See Rom 3:25.

[33] 1 Jn 3:2.

2

Demolition Troops in the Church

"Look how they hate each other!" say those on the inside and the outside who have schadenfreude as they rub their hands while watching Catholics' fratricidal war: progressives against conservatives, avant-gardists against reactionaries, or whatever they call each other. The aggression that has raged between the denominations up to now, frowned upon today due to the ecumenical wave, seems unfortunately not to have petered out but to have been cheerfully diverted to the inside. (Konrad Lorenz gave us a very clear description of the zoological aspect of this process.[1]) What used to be called a church newsletter is now often no longer used for basic edification but sees itself instead as a device for brash combat, tirelessly dredging up the last remnants of trust, reverence, and gratitude to the Church, authority, and Tradition. Staid women's magazines do not miss an opportunity to score points against the pope over the encyclical[2] and, in general, to expose the spiritual stupidity of our ancestors while complaining mildly. Not to mention the "upscale" Catholic publications. What Friedrich Heer recently called the "Nicodemic" strategy—he should know!—to

[1] Görres is likely referring to Konrad Lorenz, *On Aggression*, trans. Marjorie Kerr Wilson (New York: Bantam Books, 1966).

[2] "The encyclical" is almost certainly a reference to Pope Paul VI's controversial 1968 encyclical *Humanae vitae*, which Görres considered "a great prophetic act". See chapter 6, p. 160.

serve dynamite wrapped in orthodox vocabulary is hardly necessary.[3] What is left in the Creed that cannot be attacked directly and without any camouflage, by anybody and in any tone? Angry old men do not make the atmosphere better by insisting on a certain terminology that is already sinking into oblivion and measuring everything against it, unwilling or unable to deduce old Truth in a new guise; likewise, their skillfully placed blame of unctuous appeals for "peace in the Church" come off as quite provocative. In this way, dialogue—highly praised, recommended by all—becomes more and more difficult for both sides.

And the Catholic fratricidal struggle is not only burrowing into intellectual and journalistic realms. As in France during the Dreyfus affair, families and groups of friends are divided. Long-time colleagues, who have collaborated most of their lives, avoid one another, eyeing each other suspiciously from afar, interpreting every utterance as hostile. In unavoidable encounters, one contorts one's way frantically

[3] Görres attributes the idea of a "Nicodemic strategy" to Austrian historian Friedrich Heer. Heer writes that in "the art of Nicodemism . . . dangerous thoughts, dangerous allusions to topical ecclesiastical and political affairs, and above all to ideas hard or impossible to reconcile with the dogma of the Church or the maxims of the prevailing theology, were clothed in symbolical and allegorical forms and put into the mouths of classical poets". Friedrich Heer, *The Medieval World: Europe, 1100–1350* (London: Weidenfeld and Nicolson, 1993), 89. This was first published in German in 1961.

According to American historian Perez Zagorin, the term "Nicodemism . . . derives from 'Nicodemites,' the name the reformer John Calvin gave the crypto-Protestants and members of underground churches in Catholic lands who betrayed their faith by conforming outwardly to Catholic rites. Its origin lay in the Gospel of John, which depicts the Pharisee Nicodemus as a believer in Christ who from fear of the Jews concealed his faith and came to hear Jesus only secretly by night"; it is considered a form of "religiously motivated dissimulation." Perez Zagorin, *Ways of Lying: Dissimulation, Persecution, and Conformity in Early Modern Europe* (Cambridge, Mass.: Harvard University Press, 1990), 12.

into a conversation about neutral topics, sidestepping the hot-button issues, such as celibacy, *Humani generis*, and the Dutch Catechism [of 1966], because a dispute would lead to an open rupture.[4]

And if you really care about the fate of your beloved Church, you think anxiously of the saying: "A house divided cannot stand"[5]—something the enemies all around know by way of political instinct even without recalling biblical stories. They wait calmly.

Forty years ago, we discovered with passion that "We are the Church"; we—not just the clergy, the hierarchy, not just the past.[6] Romano Guardini spoke of the awakening of the Church in souls.[7] Today, once again, there is a danger of death in souls[8] because that sentence, isolated as a slogan,

[4] *Humani generis* is an encyclical promulgated by Pope Pius XII in 1950. The "Dutch Catechism", as it is known, was the first catechism after the Second Vatican Council. It was published in Dutch in 1966, and its content was highly controversial. It was translated into German in 1968 and into English in 1967. Hoger Katechetisch Instituut, *A New Catechism: Catholic Faith for Adults*, trans. Kevin Smyth (New York: Herder and Herder, 1967).

[5] See Mk 3:25.

[6] "Forty years ago" refers to the German Catholic Youth Movement in the 1920s and 1930s, in which Görres played an active role.

[7] "The Awakening of the Church in Souls" was the famous title of an article by Father Romano Guardini in a journal associated with the Catholic Youth Movement. Romano Guardini, "Das Erwachen der Kirche in der Seele", *Hochland* 19 (1922): 257–67.

[8] This echoes Görres' statement in an essay she wrote in 1947 in response to turmoil unleashed by her controversial 1946 "Letter on the Church". She wrote in 1947, "There is the 'awakening of the Church in souls'. There is also the 'dying of the Church in souls'." Ida Friederike Görres, "Das Gespräch über die Kirche", pt. 2, *Frankfurter Hefte* 2, no. 3 (1947): 280. The opening part of this essay about "the dying of the Church in souls" is available in

is often reduced merely to contemporaries, detached from the enormous historical structure that is rooted in the days of the Apostles and awaits the Day of Judgment and that alone may lay claim to the label "Church". The foliage of a single summer cannot determine the lifespan of an old tree, nor can it judge and reject the tree's previous development. The law according to which it has taken its place is not in its leaves. But many contemporaries, unconsciously succumbing to the existentialist idea of free human self-determination, also transfer this to the Church and dream of her total transformation based on transient trends.

For the younger generation, this does not mean revolution, not even rebellion. It only expresses the zeitgeist, which simply no longer has any relation to the past, not even necessarily a hostile one. Where should the younger ones get such a relation from? Their environment is reminiscent of the contourless, flowing, floating island world in C. S. Lewis' science fiction novel *Perelandra*; everything is changeable and is supposed to be that way; even the landscape is continuously reshaped. These generations were born in ruins and grew up in makeshift housing; they were born into a consumer milieu that is geared toward waste and discarding. They live largely among elders who pay homage to a grotesque mimicking of being young. The past confronts them predominantly in figures of the dead—as ruins, fossils, mummies, antiquities, curiosities. How are they supposed to have an

---

English in Görres' preface to Görres, *The Church in the Flesh*, vii–viii. Jennifer S. Bryson has prepared a translation of the full essay from 1947 for a forthcoming book.

eye, a feeling, for the phenomenon of a *living* permanence, a weathered yet indestructible endurance, a vitality that is not exhausted in the span of a year but, due to its multigenerational nature, requires a greater extent of time in order to express itself? They also lack the other model in which time, maturation, and duration can come into the picture in a meaningful way only by belonging to a superior complete lifespan. But both belong to the Church: a great past, a continuation as part of a great whole.

Is it any wonder when these young people no longer want to be heirs and can no longer imagine anything "worth inheriting"?

But they do not even know the extent to which they are heirs,[9] anyway. "When the future is barred to them, the admirable past may be a solace for the ills of the moribund, the sickly, the prisoner. . . . But we want no part of it."[10] "We will destroy the museums, libraries, academies of every kind."[11] A call by the extraparliamentary opposition against the cultural establishment? Not at all; rather, it is a quote from the manifesto of the Italian Futurists from 1909, five years before the First World War, when most of those who were cultured were still equated with "old" and "venerable". The zeitgeist flows out of multiple legacies—even within the Church.

"What was silent in the father speaks in the son; and often I found the son in the unveiled secret of the father";

[9] There appears to be a typographical error in the German text here. It reads "Erden" (meaning "earths"); I am reading the text as "Erben" (heirs).

[10] Filippo Tommaso Marinetti, "The Founding and Manifesto of Futurism", in *Marinetti's Selected Writings*, trans. R.W. Flint (New York: Farrar, Straus and Giroux, 1972), 19–24. First published in *Le Figaro* (Paris), February 20, 1909, 292.

[11] Marinetti, "Futurism", 291.

"aggrieved conceit, repressed envy—perhaps the conceit and envy of your fathers—erupt from you as a flame and as the frenzy of revenge."[12] Nietzsche knew this. And this is true not only in the generation gap of blood relations but also of the spirit.

How much secret unbelief, reluctantly concealed—even by priests!—now takes up oxygen inside the Church—as a painful, unsavory self-cleansing of the Church Body, like a body ridding itself of deep-rooted poisons through bursting abscesses and ugly skin rashes. How many old bills are now being settled in the Church—endlessly piled up *ressentiment*; silent grudges, having been choked back, are spewing forth. Here one really can speak of an uprising; those carrying it out are dissatisfied priests of the middle and older strata, to whom the youngest ones only provide faithful and often strangely uncritical allegiance. They are really emigrants from the past as from a land of bondage that they loathed. Civil wars have always been fueled by the impetus of private revenge.

We do not throw stones. Such people are not just troublemakers. Much real guilt of the older Church faces judgment here: overreach by the guardians of the faith in the modernist dispute and its aftereffects, blind despotic oppression, prevention of necessary improvements, infinite untruthfulness by the superficial powers that be. To this extent, so much that is ugly and embarrassing about this eruption process is both liberating and healing. It is better for the spirits to part than for fifth columns to move undetected among us.

People vary. Some forgive their parents more easily than other people, some with more difficulty. And the aftermath

[12] Friedrich Nietzsche, *Thus Spoke Zarathustra: A Book for All and None*, trans. Walter Kaufmann (New York: Penguin Books, 1978), 100.

of disappointed love is proverbial. Have we not gone through this enough times in politics?

~

The Council was a great, auspicious sowing; now we see many dismaying things sprouting up, poisonous things that threaten to choke the first fruit. Indeed, weeds often grow lavishly, much more impressively than the usual bland green of the annual harvest. But the actual new harvest can likewise sometimes look like weeds.

I confess that I am constantly wondering how exactly the Church will endure the saying "don't rip it out; instead let it grow until the harvest" during this decade.[13] Let us hope that it happens out of loyalty to the gospel and not due to the weakness of being perplexed—or at least from a mixture of both. We are not used to this; we are rather accustomed to the previous tactic of relentlessly tracking down and eradicating any microscopically suspicious new development. But was not that also a variation of the zeitgeist that was afraid of bacteria, which had repercussions in other realms, in the peculiar but very complex phenomenon of prudery and political censorship of the nineteenth century? Of course, the patience to wait demands a great deal—not just nerves and humor but also a particularly alert attention to actual movements of the Spirit of God in what is unfamiliar: for it is clear that what is really new can never be expressed clearly and correctly at first sight, but only awkwardly, contradictingly, and out of proportion, only groping for form and language. What readiness to interpretive goodwill this demands from the observer, who is offended or frightened by the hulking mass of that which is unformed!

[13] See Mt 13:24–29.

~

Nietzsche's statement about fathers and sons has other facets: "They bring to light what was hidden in their grandfathers and what their grandfathers themselves did not suspect. Often the son already betrays his father—and the father understands himself better after he has a son."[14] This also applies in a positive way—because the earlier ones were not just "growing volcanoes that approach the hour of their eruption"; rather, "all of us harbor concealed gardens and plantings."[15] And is it not actually the "natural" mandate of descendants to be the fulfillment of such divinized longings?

The Council has given to some of them air to breathe and space to live for that which, a few decades ago, floated like a specter only in small circles of farsighted youth: the secular institutes, the worker priests, the ecumenical wave, the conversation with socialism, the encounter with Islam, Buddhism, Hinduism.

The plant world offers us other analogies. Every spring shows us the spectacle of the journey of the amaryllis, which is almost dismaying for an unsuspecting observer: from dry, woodlike bulbs into the glorious blaze of crisscrossing scarlet trumpets. Who should reject such a result as a symptom of disease? But who, conversely, should reject the stalk and protective capsule as superfluous, hindering deformations? Those of us who are older must therefore be prepared for legitimate surprises in the change in the shape of the Church even if she simply detonates and throws away a lot of things that we ourselves have helped to shape with the ardent commitment of our lives. What looks more pathetic than a with-

[14] Friedrich Nietzsche, *The Gay Science*, trans. Walter Kaufmann (New York: Vintage Books, 1974), 83.

[15] Nietzsche, *The Gay Science*, 84.

ered, tattered bud cover? But would the flower have matured without it?

Last summer, on an empty ocean beach, when the tide came in during the morning, I had an opportunity to watch how the high tide, pressing forward ripple by ripple, often came up to the most beautiful sandcastles from the previous day. It swished around, poured into, eroded, and disintegrated them until they were unrecognizable. No subsequent ebb tide left them visible. We have lived in an ebbing of the Church for a very long time. Now a rising spiritual high tide roars in, slowly and irresistibly; it is a time of rejoicing and a threat at the same time. The Youth Movement, too, was an early, singular advance that has long since been overwhelmed by a more powerful surge. Will not this current flood reveal much to be "sandcastles" that at the time—and earlier—appeared to us as "built for eternity"?

But the same landscape also displayed the dams and levees by which a population wages a large-scale, heroic defense against the seemingly absolutely overwhelming ocean tide just when it wants to eat away the ground under their feet, the bedrock of life. We must learn to distinguish.

The big real estate developer, it seems, wants to redesign his city. This includes demolition and letting things disappear. He does not ask the old buildings' inhabitants, for whom every stone is soaked with memories, who have their whole hearts built into the structure of these walls, about this. The inhabitants are better suited for tending to the blueprints, for drawing up plans, and perhaps later for helping to build. For the first stage of work, he brings in strangers, rough journeymen who proceed with explosives and picks without hesitation, respect, or piety, for whom a stone is simply a stone. Perhaps it cannot be otherwise, unless bombs, earthquakes, floods provide the same service—they, too, are tools of God; who can deny that? Nobody can demand that we be disposed favorably even to the people who are called to dig the graves, to do the clearing out, who perhaps even enjoy it. But lowering mountains and exalting valleys to prepare the way of the Lord is, after all, just a more poetic expression for such an endeavor.[16] It does not go off without a lot of noise and dirt, without the devastation of a beloved landscape, burying villages, and building drainage systems. The gifts are as different as the tasks. We cannot be monument protectors and iconoclasts rolled into one.

But even the providentially appointed demolition crew must not just embark wildly, not even to do what we, for a thousand reasons, would be unable to do. They require strict, vigilant supervision and often resolute resistance. We could not prevent any of the air raids, which, in the end, also lay in the incomprehensible will of God's Providence; but by ardently, carefully grabbing things, we were able to rescue for later a great deal of what was irreplaceably precious.

Of course, the debris and mess that the leveling teams create is much louder and more visible than the bashfully sprouting "concealed gardens and plantings" by which the other part—I fear much smaller part—brings about the growth of an offshoot. Our whole heart belongs to those who are busy fulfilling the unredeemed promises of our youth,[17] who are awakening and shaping the dormant pos-

[16] See Is 40:4.

[17] Görres is referring here to her experiences in the Catholic Youth Movement.

sibilities of the Church. For them—and not just for them!—we must preserve the old, the retired, the blueprints, and the seeds that are slipping away into being forgotten today. Perhaps already the generation after next will be tired of their own fathers' delight in destruction and will look for material to build the bridge of time between the past and their present. Development is not as straightforward and single-track as one would like; rather, it happens in zigzags and spirals. At the next bend, that which is old and true must be present again, clear and tangible for the seeker, not ground up in a garbage chute. "The intellectual-spiritual segment of cable may have to be laid above or below ground—to secure the rights to pass on tradition against and independent of the ruling power of the era; this is an eternal imperative of the hour," says Eugen Rosenstock-Huessy.

This seems to be entrusted primarily to two transmitters: the ecclesial-papal Magisterium and the "little ones", the "common people", among the people of God. The first instance goes without saying. John Henry Newman referred to the latter in that famous *Rambler* essay that caused him serious trouble (and was recently published with a good commentary by Jean Guitton).[18] The immense turmoil of the Arian heresy of the fourth century tore apart the Church—the sons and grandsons of the martyrs!—almost into a chaos of feuding parties and sects. Even a large number of the bishops fell away from doctrine, which had only just barely been salvaged during the persecution. It was the people, the ignorant, the common folk who upheld the full faith of their

[18] John Henry Newman, "On Consulting the Faithful in Matters of Doctrine", *Rambler*, July 1859, https://newmanreader.org/works/rambler/consulting.html. The commentary that Görres mentions is Jean Guitton, *The Church and the Laity: From Newman to Vatican II*, trans. Malachy Gerard Carroll (Staten Island, N.Y.: Alba House, 1965).

fathers through thick and thin and carried it on (admittedly, their minds were not yet dulled by mass media). Newman speaks of the *sensus fidelium*, which can be translated as "the religious instinct of the faithful": "the surest instinct in discerning the mysteries of which the Holy Spirit breathes the grace through the Church, and who, with as sure a tact, reject what is alien from her teaching",[19] and manifests itself in the life of prayer, in devotions, customs, and liturgy (which has not yet been forced into line with being just a matter for a commission!).

It is probably the same as what is meant with the little ones to whom the Father reveals what He is hiding from those who are overly clever—as long as the little ones are pure of heart and not just an amplifying echo chamber for those super-clever ones who make public opinion in the Church at present, as in politics.

In this crisis, unfortunately, it seems we can rely far less on the professional theologians, whether priests or laypeople. Julien Benda's gloomy expression of the "betrayal by the intellectuals" (*trahison des clercs*) seems to have acquired a fatal perpetual validation.[20] With a few exceptions, they seem to be more susceptible to seduction by the addiction to innovation at any price, by ambition and vanity, sensationalism, and competition for celebrity status—in short, what Clemens Brentano called "those trying to woo the spirit of the times", occasionally seduced even by an excessive, pitiful identification with error. So, one cannot take in their utterance other than with the utmost wariness and wait-and-see caution, let alone accept it. Where does one

[19] This is a quotation from the bishop of Birmingham cited by Newman in "On Consulting the Faithful".

[20] Julien Benda, *The Betrayal of the Intellectuals*, trans. Richard Aldington (Boston: Beacon Press, 1969). First published in French 1927.

sense something of emphatic respect for the conscience of the "little ones", of readiness to make ultimate sacrifices for the unity of the Church?

Yet the Church should not become an intergenerational battlefield; she should rather "be a union of generations who look at each other, do not turn their backs on each other—where the forefather speaks for the grandson, the grandchildren speak for the forefathers". Thus Eugen Rosenstock-Huessy again, the Jewish thinker and Protestant Christian.

We heard a strangely beautiful and moving reading on the Saturday after Ash Wednesday:

> And you shall be like a watered garden, like a spring of water, whose waters do not fail. And your ancient ruins shall be rebuilt; you shall raise up the foundations of many generations; you shall be called the repairer of the breach, the restorer of streets to dwell in.[21]

The Church today faces indictment, judgment, confession, repentance, and reparation. God is gracious to the penitent, and the sign of grace is the hope that this prophetic Word promises to the one who repents.

[21] Is 58:11–12.

3

Faith: Skeleton or Body?

At a meal, a husband asks, "Which butcher do we buy from?" The wife replies, "Since when do you not like the meat?" The punchline of this simple joke applies not only in the domestic realm. Some who raise the philosophical, objective question "Is there a hierarchy of truths?" would be served less well by a tract suitable for schoolchildren (which I could not even write) than by the simple counterquestion: "So then, which doctrine would you like to see ranked lowest?"

We have to become more and more attentive to the often matted web of motives and intentions that tangles itself around apparently innocuous academic questions, especially regarding religious and ecclesiastical problems.

A hierarchy of truths? Does that even exist? Is there not only one Truth, as there is only one "health", and only an examination separates it into manageable strands?

The question of a hierarchy of truths has always existed in the Church. It was not invented by the Second Vatican Council, as one reads with astonishment more and more often, nor was it legitimized by it. It is inevitable with religious reflection—because the communicated Truth of God is limitless and inexhaustible; the human mind receiving it is narrow and limited in its attention span. Ever since the believer has considered what he has received, this relationship has troubled him. He has expressed it in many images and parables: the one light and the many rays; core and shell; tree with roots, trunk, and leaves; center and growth rings; destination and paths; and so on.

Christian theology must, from the very start, structure the content of faith and demarcate it from nonbinding opinions as well as from hostile errors: first, by way of mystagogy, in degrees of initiation, baptismal creeds, liturgical formulas, scriptural canon; in missionizing and educating; polemically in wrestling with heresies; and academically. From the Middle Ages on, increasingly detailed tables of refined qualifications regarding the obligation to believe and regarding credibility, from revelation and dogma to "tolerated opinion", emerge. At the universities, making such qualifications was part of the routine of theological work. Such gradations were already upheld by Albertus Magnus.

In modern times, the institution became more and more of a precision scale for orthodoxy. In monitoring doctrine and writings, it was adjusted to register the most imperceptible deviations, to the point of the most finicky pedantry, and, combined with policing methods, it was also a serious stumbling block for theological development within the Church.

Of course, this has vanished like a ghost in our time. The equally concerning antithesis is already on display. Is there, one asks oneself, still a binding norm of orthodoxy, even for the responsible guardians of the truths of the faith? Current theological activity does not exactly thrust this impression onto an observer. The silence of the Magisterium dismays the faithful, who are facing the merrily rampant spread of heresies of all shades. Is the silence an expression of anxious perplexity—or are we witnessing a theatrical performance quite unusual in Church history: "Let the Weeds Grow Until the Harvest"?[1]

Only in discussions of ecumenical rapprochement and in some fields of moral theology do we still find an effort to set boundaries and distinctions.

The "pre-conciliar" layman had little interest in the intellectual problem of gradations of truth. On the whole, he believed the whole and in the whole and confidently left the nuance to the theological experts, according to the principle "Better to believe too much than too little!" Today, this attitude is condemned in thick books as shameful intellectual laziness, immaturity, infantile submissiveness in the face of authoritarian despotism toward opinions. This accusation overshoots the mark and misses the point. Until recently, religion usually meant to the layman *doing, first*, then knowing the theory. For the one who was lukewarm, it was a sum of "religious duties" to be performed willingly or unwillingly; for the pious one, a way of life—what is today called "spirituality". Thus, the interest in learning, asking questions, dissecting, discovering (which certainly existed!) was focused not on dogmatics but on the "spiritual life": the Commandments as "the imperative form of truth", morality, asceticism, prayer, good works, striving for Christian perfection—even including

[1] Görres is playing off the parable of the weeds among the wheat (Mt 13:24–30). In that parable, Jesus says, "Let both grow together until the harvest" (v. 30). Görres appears to be suggesting, tongue-in-cheek, that in the new "theatrical performance", the weeds should be not only tolerated but *allowed* to "grow . . . until the harvest" (but as for the wheat, that is not so clear).

tinkering and systematization, with associated, amazingly extensive literature for every level.

The passionate awakening of theological interest in lay circles in the 1920s was under the same auspices: knowledge as a precious segment of "life with God", the inexhaustible source of tradition and history for personal and ecclesial renewal—for the whole, within the whole.

~

After all, "hierarchy" signifies a *sacred* order, with real—not imaginary, not playful—tiers. But these arise only in and out of a context, presupposing a "body of faith" (*Glaubenskörper*) as Möhler calls it, an inherently secure and unshakable unity, while open to infinite growth. It is only within this that each part has its place and character in inexhaustible points of contact, correspondences, complements, interdependencies, and interactions with all the parts. No individual truth can be "interrogated" (that is what certain present-day investigative attitudes must be called) in isolation; none yields its true meaning when torn out, and none can justify its existence separately. Not even, for example, the message of brotherly love. Could it not be just a pipe dream, an illusion, a propagandistic slogan? Only the whole justifies itself in its existence.

This whole is the faith of the *Church*, which we do not understand as the statistical sum of Catholics now living but, rather, as the phenomenon of a unique kind that she is, far transcending her tangible sociological, psychological, and historical shells—the Church, reaching from the days of the Apostles up to the Second Coming of Christ, with her own consciousness, self-understanding, and law of development. The faith of the Church radiates out into individual believers like the life of the body into its cells. It far surpasses individual consciousness, just as theology does, just as the mystery surpasses word and formula, the unseparated surpasses the knowable. We live in our faith more than the faith in us. Newman sketched an impressive image of this:

> [A cosmos of faith,] a vast system, not to be comprised in a few sentences, not to be embodied in one code or treatise, but consisting of a certain body of Truth, pervading the Church like an atmosphere, irregular in its shape from its very profusion and exuberance; at times separate only in idea from Episcopal Tradition, yet at times melting away into legend and fable; partly written, partly unwritten, partly the interpretation, partly the supplement of Scripture, partly preserved in intellectual expressions, partly latent in the spirit and temper of Christians; poured to and fro in closets and upon the housetops, in liturgies, in controversial works, in obscure fragments, in sermons, in popular prejudices, in local customs.[2]

Such faith is not abstract but concrete—and something concrete (*concretum*) is, after all, something that has coalesced, a mixed entity. Of course, it also has weak parts—ephemeral, corrupted, and replaceable—that nevertheless belong to it like the leaves to the tree, which the tree sprouts and sheds. Abundance always contains superfluous things,

[2] John Henry Newman, *An Essay on the Development of Christian Doctrine* (London: Longmans, Green, 1909), 76–77, https://www.newmanreader.org/works/development/index.html. Görres has "a cosmos of faith" ("Ein Glaubenskosmos") in the quotation marks with the rest of the quote, but I did not find a word or phrase like "cosmos of faith" in or near this passage from Newman. Also, it is interesting to observe that this quotation in the German text appears to be Görres' translation from the English; she does not quote from the established German translation of this work, namely, John Henry Kardinal Newman, *Die Entwicklung der christlichen Lehre und der Begriff der Entwicklung*, trans. Theodor Haecker (Munich: Verlag Hermann A. Weichmann, 1922), 75–76.

just as our food contains ballast. Who would want to live on pure nutritional infusions?

In contrast, a "naked" theology seems to want to assert itself today, "information" that is solely literal and conceptual, and then pure action derived from this, without an intermediate "spiritual life" and without the surging waters of the medium of tradition: with itself as the supreme authority of faith in the face of the "cosmos of faith" that is discarded as a tangled mass and a heap of clutter. It is a skeleton without a body, and not even a whole skeleton—because it also carves out the thin slice of the present from the trunk with its growth rings, and once more, out of this, it carves out the opinions of one doctrinal party. This devastating lack of breadth and substance has to play up specialist fringe output to give itself face and weight, such as individual exegetical-philological hypotheses against the central, original dogmas. Serving people is placed above serving God, the category of unconditional skepticism above trust and obedience. Political social "dogmas", as the normative standard, simply eliminate conflicting truths of faith. What has been rejected should be concealed even from children; in religious education, their natural dispositions to deeper reception of faith—reverence, reserve, generosity, and trust—should be suppressed or even destroyed.

In the age of depth psychology, everyone ought to know what repressed truths can do subliminally; even a community cannot silence its past or important contents of consciousness with impunity. Church history shows clearly enough how banished elements return in the form of internal conflicts, in the form of heresies, falsifying the elements of Truth with foreign alloys, allying them to hostile powers.

~

Only the whole can decide which truths are vital to it and how they are supported and nourished by what is less important, which also has its functions. Only what is living can determine what is flesh versus what is clothing, what would be an operation necessary for healing versus what would be mutilation. The Church has her own organ for such decisions: the Magisterium—even if the word has also become a red flag to many—and the sense of faith of the faithful [*sensus fidelium*]. The many can and must bring content and suggestions, urge and warn; the final word does not rest with them, and a theology inspired and mobilized by outsiders only attempts usurpation when it presumes to do so. Neither the loudness of demands nor even a majority of votes from those who are present at a moment in history is the legitimate bearer of such decisions. The world awoke and found itself Arian—that is, heretical—as the story in the fourth century goes.[3] It is conceivable that the Church—as in the countries of persecution—would even be legitimately represented by a minority that knows itself to be identical in faith with the living past and perseveres with

[3] "The world awoke and found itself Arian" is a version of the famous quote by St. Jerome, "The whole world groaned, and was astonished to find itself Arian". Jerome, "The Dialogue Against the Luciferians", in *A Select Library of Nicene and Post-Nicene Fathers of the Christian Church, Second Series*, eds. Philip Schaff and Henry Wace (New York: The Christian Literature Company, 1893), 6:329.

the pope and bishops in harmony, and thus as one and the same as her historical character.

~

In addition to the Christian doctrinal order of valid truths, there is always a different kind of "hierarchy of Truth"—an [internally] manifold one—that is practical, subjective, completely legitimate. I would like to call it the "biographical" one. It follows simply from the nature of human limitation in the face of the overflowing fullness of the divine claim. None of us can respond to all of our knowledge about our faith at once. How revealing are answers to the question "What do you think is the most important thing about Christianity?" Finding God, who is gracious; information about life after death; covenant with God; worship of God; the kingdom of God; brotherly love—as varied as the answers to the initial question in instruction for converts: "Why do you want to become Catholic?"

How could it be any different? There are truths from the first and second half of life that one does not perceive at the same time, just as a landscape in different lighting shows completely different details. There is nearness and distance, openness and reticence toward certain truths, varying even according to constitution and situation. Some "speak to us" directly, others remain silent; we "cannot do anything with them" without disputing or denying them. This does not make them less true and important. Truths are our pungent medicine or our daily bread, a flotation device thrown to us or a weight-bearing floor we do not notice. Biographies and hagiographies tell of a conversion in a flash or a dispatch to a mission like a burst of fire, through a single word of Scripture. Many are seed and leaven for us, as the Gospel explicitly says.[4] There are typical as well as fatefully unrepeatable circumstances. Who would be allowed to decide which can be "dispensed" with? Truths lie in us like eyes, like lungs in the embryo; only in the next phase of existence does their meaning reveal itself—or their absence reveals itself as a calamity.

This biographical order of Truth applies not only to the individual but also to the Church. One could write her interior history according to the change of these guiding stars, which often shaped an entire age creatively, as the Passion of the Lord and eschatology shaped the Middle Ages.

All these transformations are good—our only possibility of development!—as long as the truth of the hour, personal or historical, is not played out like a weapon to degrade the others, to erase the background. In this, wanting to "abolish" is nonsense and sacrilege. Behind such storming in and impugning, however, there is often something else that must be more important to us. The disorientation of the world that is disturbed by turmoil cries out in wild impatience for help, and it punches and kicks at everything that does not immediately bring help or that seems to bypass it. This need is badly served by bootlicking compliance, which takes the wording of the attacks too seriously and which, in a defeatist manner—in order not to irritate anyone—wants to conceal everything in the proclamation that is not immediately and effortlessly grasped by everyone, whatever does not "suit" them. Here Talleyrand is right: "Only that which resists can support." Only in the strict and gentle preservation of the ancient, eternal hierarchy of the truth of revelation can the Church offer that help which does not negate time but, rather, fulfills it.

[4] Lk 13:18–21.

We who are older have to develop a seismographic sensitivity in our hearing in order to be able to infer, beneath the ongoing uproar, the deeper underlying intention, the enormous struggle of the era, which circles the old truths in some people—but they are the ones who matter!—hungry for the eternal images, people whose cloudy mirrors the era furiously smashes.

~

But realms of time are not figures of speech; they are rather real like realms of land and air. The Church, the ancient hierarchical houselike structure, holds many of them under her roofs. But each realm also has its own language, often different from the language of tribes and peoples. And every idiom is better spoken by natives than by immigrants, visitors, deportees. It is better to translate into one's own language than out of it. Thus, the era's new robe, made out of the old Truth, can be manufactured only by children whose origins in the new epoch are authentic, who are connected to their predecessors by lineage and by Tradition that cannot be broken. They already exist, the true heirs, the shapers of tomorrow's Church, the spokespersons for her future, not just a defensive rearguard. They exist even among theologians. To them, as to the silent people among the faithful and the faithful shepherds, belong our hope and trust. Many of them may still slumber unawakened, some quietly ripening; some may still rage, like Saul, among the attackers and destroyers. God already knows them, and their hour awaits them.

We can only wish that they increase while we decrease.[5]

[5] See John 3:30: "He must increase, but I must decrease."

4

The Spirituality of Studying Theology

A Presentation Given to Lay Theologians

Among the striking features of our present era is the sudden, jarring surge of interest in religion and, with it, the attraction to the study of theology among laypeople in particular—in striking contrast to the declining number of priestly vocations.

Church history teaches us that, in times of crisis in the Church, religious and theological interest (two different interests, as we shall see later) have, like a flood, always seized broad circles of Christians—that is, it was by no means just "the bickering of monks", as scoffers each time have viewed it. During the great trinitarian and christological controversies, people argued in the markets and in the barbershops of Antioch and Alexandria as to whether the Father is equal to or greater than the Son; in the century of the Reformation, tailors and cobblers squabbled in the drinking rooms of the guilds, sometimes with "conclusive" arguments about whether faith or works bring salvation and how far the power of the pope reaches, if, by right, he has any at all.

In a historical novella, [Werner] Bergengruen describes a Christian who lives with his faith like a man with his inherited treasure chest: he knows that it contains what is most precious to him; he is willing to guard it, to defend it, if necessary, to pass it on to his children undamaged; but he never even considers opening it and examining the items individually and critically.[1] This picture probably reflects a common behavior that has been widespread for centuries, composed of various strands. There is the natural trust in the professional specialists in the most diverse areas of life, at least in those who are in authority. Everyone wears shoes; who wants to be introduced to all the details of how they are made, the study of the materials, and so on? Everyone needs a doctor from time to time; who wants to study medicine in order either to check on him or to be able to do without him? Second, this attitude was strongly endorsed and encouraged by the clergy. Theological interest—and experiment!—among the laity has been a neuralgic point for the clergy from time immemorial. After all, what else were the secret meetings (conventicles) and itinerant preachers of the various medieval heresies? The hierarchy thanked God if the layman did not show himself to be too curious in this regard but, rather, lived contentedly in possession of his treasure chest. As a counterweight to the hierarchy, the sectarian movements produced the fearful isolation of theology from clerical circles, its jealous monopolization—which, to a large extent, was also simply connected with the fact that *le clerc* (the cleric) possessed the monopoly on study and academic endeavors in general.

As for the man with the treasure chest—that is, with implicit faith, who was happy to be satisfied with the explicit, regular, as well as occasional small allocation through sermons, books, and a general life of faith—we should not,

[1] There is a remote possibility that Görres is referring to the novella *Schatzgräbergeschichte*; however, the storyline of this tale is quite different from what she describes here. Werner Bergengruen, *Schatzgräbergeschichte* (Zurich: Arche, 1948). She is referring, more likely, to one of Bergengruen's other many novellas.

therefore, summarily ascribe laziness in thinking and dullness in faith to him today. First of all, in times when there was a general, varied, and lively "religious milieu", theology was, in a much stricter sense, only a single segment of a broadly comprehensive whole of faith that towered over theology; it really concerned only very few directly. Second, even the ordinary Christian possessed a deep organic sense of the Church, rarely encountered today, that hardly needed reflection or formulation: a genuine sense of the body [of the Church] that felt that the priest was the institutional representative on behalf of all of us, one who does not withdraw or withhold from us certain services and therefore privileges but performs them precisely "for" us, in our place and for our benefit; this was true in the liturgy as well as in theology. Only growing individualism, almost without giving it a thought, destroyed this simple and sincere relationship with the priest.

Growing education revealed to some the disconcerting discrepancy between their stuck-in-time, passive, and childlike knowledge of religion and the rest of their intellectual level. The shock of the First World War jolted many out of their accustomed indifference and led younger people in particular to confront fundamental questions about themselves.

During the 1920s, the various renewal movements within the Church awakened a powerful hunger in smaller circles for more and better knowledge and understanding of the faith: the Bible Movement, the Liturgical Movement, the academic-religious movement, and, last but not least, the Youth Movement, which eagerly soaked all this up. Looking back, one is amazed at the insatiable zeal with which young people at the time threw themselves into furthering their religious education and going deeper: Bible study evenings, liturgical evenings, discussions of dogmatics, of Church history—this happened week after week, tirelessly. Later, when under attack during the Nazi era, religiously going deeper became a vital suit of armor for those who persevered: Religious education for adults acquired a new, very serious emphasis, and after the war, it was all the more necessary that the young people, who had hardly received any religious instruction, should subsequently be given at least the basics. Today there is restlessness in the Church—already semiconsciously, subliminally pulsating and fermenting for a long time—that was awakened and articulated by the Council and gained worldwide, unprecedented publicity through mass media. In comparison, consider how long it took for the Tridentine decrees to seep through to remote areas, for the Council [of Trent] to become known at all! Through the constant information and constant discussion, through the flood of small and large changes that, as a result, swept over the Church, people—countless people—first became aware of just how minimally they were actually at home in their own faith, how little they knew about it, and how little they understood what was being negotiated worldwide, and they started digging in and continue to do so with very commendable zeal to fill in these cavernous gaps—in other words: moving from the faith of childhood or youth to an adult faith. What is new is the mass scale of this.

There is so much that is healthy and joyful, so much that is genuine in these pangs of the Spirit, in this general awakening of the thirst for religious knowledge, that the Church heartily welcomes this phenomenon and is responding to it with many different events. The former small private groups and courses have been replaced by large training institutes open to all, in-person as well as distance-learning theology courses, and an overabundance of related printed works.

But all this was and is far from being lay *theology*. There have always been *lay* theologians—individual ones—but, in a sense, that is clearly different from what this means today: Christians wanted to think through questions of faith *as* laymen, to describe these questions, to offer new insights—not only vis-à-vis the consecrated but also vis-à-vis the specialists. Great names such as Blaise Pascal, Friedrich von Hügel, Theodor Haecker, and C. S. Lewis are among them.

Today's lay theologian, however, wants to be an expert in theology, just like the priest, in order to participate like him as a "specialist", partly in the proclamation of the Church, mostly as a teacher of religion, partly to influence theological development, as an author in public media, on the radio, as an editor, even as an academic teacher.

But other, murkier drives are mixed in with the pure thirst for knowledge. On the one hand, the healthy drive that one sees in what is called the lay movement toward maturity—still a highly ambiguous concept!—is expressed here; on the other hand, there is the resentment that unfortunately also colors this movement so strongly. Some individuals no longer want any gradation of roles in the Church; they want everything "as well"; they want everything "themselves". They no longer want to be represented, neither in rituals nor in thought.

Many a believer also has the uneasy suspicion that the treasure chest contains, alongside jewels, quite a lot of useless stuff, fakes, junk that has been thoughtlessly schlepped along. He wants a clearing out, and he wants to do it himself. He does not trust that the official administrators of the overall treasure have either credible knowledge or honest will. Certainly, he has all sorts of reasons, not only occasion, for such distrust. A tremendously overstretched concept of authority, an indiscriminately frozen practical application of handing down (*tradierens*), and perhaps the most important element, a very old bitter experience of that behavior on the part of spiritual authorities that I am accustomed to call "pedagogical fraud": the manipulation of the truths of faith by exaggeration, omission, and glossing over in order to achieve quick, easy, dazzling results with the "pupil". Here, unfortunately with good reason, a tremendous readiness to be suspicious has accumulated, which wants to be legitimized and to confirm itself. Thus, many a layman would prefer to be self-sufficient in relation to Church teachers. He would at least like to be able to control—not just judge—the priest's sermon, the pastoral letter, and the content of his church bulletins on the basis of his own knowledge. He wants to keep a close eye on his "shepherds"; he wants to be able to impose his views on them and enforce them in the event of differences of opinion. Here also the leveling urge, which is so powerful in the Church today, that calls itself democratic, shows itself; it appears to me, however, much more as an expression of that "global power of envy" that sociologists are already employing as an effective motive for the public.

The priest is to be stripped of all privileges, which are now perceived as theft from the crowd, as hubris. Also, he should no longer have any special knowledge, no intellectual secret possession. There must be no more echelons and therefore no more esotericism in the Church, certainly not as a class privilege. Everyone must have the same right to the same education, no longer subject to any conditions. This also includes opening the lecture halls in the theological faculties for studies that are authentic, comprehensive, and degree granting.

And this is where the real question we have comes in: Whose university education? What do the majority of the young people who fill the seats there actually want? Do they really want to study theology, Catholic theology—or just to pursue religious studies, the history of religion, the psychology of religion in the Christian, Catholic sector?

What is the difference between these? And should not the question arise whether everyone is capable of studying theology in exactly the same way as all the other subjects that are taught there—or whether there are not certain prerequisites that speak for or against such an area of study, when it is to take place outside the priesthood? After all, every serious specialized area of study requires certain dispositional inclinations and attitudes. Indeed, this is so for "the search for knowledge" in general, even before any specialization—what Newman described very nicely in a university sermon as "the philosophical temper", as indispensable for the philosopher as for the researcher.

"Rashness of assertion, hastiness in drawing conclusions, unhesitating reliance on our own acuteness and powers of reasoning, are inconsistent with the homage" that is, reverence,[2] "which nature exacts of those who would know her hidden wonders. . . . To be dispassionate and cautious, to be fair in discussion, to give to each phenomenon which nature successively presents its due weight, candidly to admit those which militate against our own theory, to be willing to be ignorant for a time, to submit to difficulties, and

[2] The word "homage" in Newman's text is translated as *Ehrfurcht* in the German text. Elsewhere in this essay, I translate *Ehrfurcht* as "reverence". *Ehrfurcht* is a central concept for Görres in this essay; thus, it is important to see how this passage from Newman relates to other ways Görres employs the term "reverence" in this essay.

patiently and meekly proceed . . ."[3] All of this is an essential basic disposition. There are also special gifts. For example, Georg Volk's essay that is far too little known, "On the Doctor and the Sick", compiles the prerequisites for a medical practitioner with impressive clarity: passion for concrete, precise, and comprehensive knowledge, tenacious zeal for constant further education, sensory sharpness that is applied and constantly being trained, the ability to sympathize and to master the sympathetic currents, and many other things.[4]

Thus, the biologist and the physicist must possess an above-average disposition, or at least a willingness, to be patient, reliable, and thorough to withstand the endless series of tedious and often-fruitless experiments, and they must possess an enormously sensitive conscientiousness never to suppress the slightest undesirable result out of laziness or for the sake of a pet theory, and so forth.

What, then, are we looking for in the theologian in terms of ethical and religious "special gear"? Does he need any at all? Can one (to use an expression that is unpleasant but now fashionable and in use) speak of a personal *spirituality of the theology student*, alongside and apart from what we have just called the basic attitude of "searching for knowledge" in general?

I think so. Whoever wants to make thinking about God, talking about God, the central content of his life requires

[3] John Henry Newman, "Sermon 1. The Philosophical Temper, First Enjoined by the Gospel", in *Fifteen Sermons Preached before The University of Oxford* (London: Longmans, Green, 1909), 8–10, https://www.newmanreader.org/works/oxford/sermon1.html.

[4] Georg Volk, *Vom Arzt und vom Kranken*, Veröffentlichung des Beuroner Arbeitskreises (Freiburg: Alber, 1949). Volk delivered this lecture on September 15, 1948. The mention of "the sympathetic currents" likely refers to homeopathy, which was an area of Volk's medical practice.

dispositions that are at least as well defined as those of the chemist and the historian.

Now, do not be alarmed when the answer puts some of the most unpopular words, almost subjected to a new taboo, onto the table: the theologian should be pious, believing, humble, pure of heart, in constant loving union with God and His Church.

Are these truisms? Not at all. For many Christians, or those who call themselves such, these words are clumps of mold from a storage chest or fossils to which the reaction is only boredom or amusement. Yet we must examine them for their original and full meaning.

It is precisely today that the theologian needs these qualities, which were by no means merely suitable as embellishment in staid intellectual-spiritual peacetime but would be superfluous and useless today—today, when theology has quite explicitly become a construction site, a battlefield, and a laboratory. On the contrary, today they are of *existential importance* as a compass, a "nose", as an organ for orientation, to catch a scent, and to weigh, as an organ that finds its way through, even where the massive signposts are falling over and sinking.

There is a composition on which every religion of the world is based, from which each one is nourished, from the loss of which each one dies. And even if, according to a popular way of thinking, "Christianity" does not belong to the "religions" (which, well, makes sense from a very specific perspective), in the Christian relationship with God, it is certainly not possible to build on a different spiritual foundation. I would like to call it "reverence syndrome": consisting of reverence, devotion, obedience, loyalty, and gratitude to the Deity and to what is considered the Deity's legitimate representation. The unity is so dense that the individual features can be separated only theoretically and analytically; they behave more like the colors of a prism than strands in a textile.

It is clear that its value as a whole rests not in itself but, rather, *in the Counterpart to which it relates*, for it is completely and entirely "re-sponse," correspondence, relationship. Therefore, as something ambivalent, like everything human, it always hovers in danger of falling into usurpation. Committed to "idols" instead of to God, in every sense, in a political, social, aesthetic, as well as religious sense: this belongs to the most threatening forces of destruction. It is equally clear that, even within the Christian faith, it can quietly and imperceptibly shift its object: from God to His representatives, from Truth to formula, from what is permanent to what is merely the past, from content to form. These possibilities and their tragic realization also explain (but only very partially!) some of the widespread and sweeping discrediting of "reverence syndrome" in our world. Nevertheless, whatever its distortions and excesses, it remains the core of every relationship with God, the essence of piety.

It occurs in different aggregate states, so to speak: as down-to-earth, unconscious, collective, as a solid, hardly noticed reason for life, or as a diffuse atmosphere. It rises into consciousness only at certain heights or unsettling periods of life. It is what we inaccurately usually call childish piety, inherited piety, or popular piety.

Second, it occurs individualized, as a reflection or groping for reflection, in the fluid state of experience, movement, activity, zeal, woe; it is that *love* for God—come on, let us call it that openly!—that is expressed gladly and willingly in deed, prayer, educating oneself, worship; usually combined with religious interest or religious aptitude, or both, neither of which, however, is identical with or indispensable to piety.

Third, it occurs in the ardent, fiery state of *passion for God*, which is expressed positively as holiness, negatively as fanaticism. We know there are impious theologians—intellectually they are stiff iron, empirically they are present. Not just today. The figure of Abbé Cénabre depicted by Bernanos in *Under the Sun of Satan* is unforgettable: a specialist in mysticism and mystical texts, also an atheist and given over to the Evil One.[5] Of course, one can approach the material of theology out of mere intellectual or psychological curiosity, irreverently, ungratefully, cynically, without a will to make orderly sense of it, with distrust and suspicion of those working in the field of theology. And it seems self-evident to me that especially a study of theology in this state can increase unbelief to the point of enmity toward God; for it offers fodder in abundance for all negative reactions. A [Church] office can even be used to destroy "reverence syndrome" in the hearers, to awaken and nurture habitual distrust of authority, mocking others, resentment, habitual ingratitude toward what has been received—in other words: damaging, perhaps destroying, the natural *capacitas Dei* (capacity for God) in souls in many ways—a sacrilege with incalculable consequences.

But the person doing this—is he actually doing theology? Is not the name itself a presumption? Does not an impious theologian, a cynical theologian, violate his own justification to exist, like a doctor who kills, a watchman who sleeps, a pharmacist who poisons? Is he a "theologian" at all, or is he just a scholar of religion working with Christian material,

[5] Georges Bernanos, *Under the Sun of Satan*, trans. Harry Lorin Binsse (Providence: Cluny Media, 2017).

who lacks the actual aptitude for what he is studying, without which he cannot even get a proper perspective on the phenomenon? After all, theology is *fides quaerens intellectum* (faith seeking understanding)—not intellect that coldly and detachedly, perhaps hostilely, dissects the object of "faith". Theology is the unfolding of the Logos in faith's understanding of itself; it is the Church's constant reflection on her own faith. Theology can be done only from within.

Now, it is, admittedly, a professional temptation of theologians to confuse knowledge with faith, faith with knowledge; knowledge—that is, gnosis, formally, not in terms of content. Such a person considers his own assent, on the basis of his own investigation, to be faith as a result of knowledge, effort, and right thinking: *credo quia intelligam* (I believe because I understand). He considers Christian faith to be a variety of scientific conviction in the subject of religion. "Yes, that is the way it is, because I have examined it and seen it" is his final verdict. "If, based on my thinking, I arrived at opinions that differed from the Church, I would consider them valid." "Private judgment", the purely individual formation of opinions in matters of faith, is what Newman, the great intellectual of the highest order, fought all his life as the actual root of all unbelief.[6] For faith does

[6] In 1874, Newman wrote, "For the benefit of some Catholics I would observe that, while I acknowledge one Pope, *jure divino*, I acknowledge no other; and that I think it a usurpation too wicked to be comfortably dwelt upon, when individuals use their own private judgement in the discussion of religious questions for the purpose of anathematizing the private judgement of others. I say there is only one Oracle of God, the Holy Catholic Church, and the Pope as her head. To her teaching I have ever desired all my thoughts, all my words, to be conformed; to her judgment I submit what I have now written, what I have ever written, not only as regards its truth, but as to its prudence, its suitableness and its expedience." John Henry Newman, "A Letter Addressed to the Duke of Norfolk on Occasion of Mr. Gladstone's Recent Expostulation", in *Certain Difficulties Felt by Anglicans in Catholic Teaching* (London: Longmans, Green & Co., 1900), 2:346–47.

not come about as a "monadic" act of an individual but, rather, happens *between* two: the One who offers and the one who accepts and concurs. There is no such thing as a monopolar faith, a mere "opinion" committed only to itself. All faith believes *someone*—namely, God, Christ, the Church.

(Incidentally, there is, of course, no self-sufficient understanding in other areas either, above all in science. The mathematician must also first accept the symbols; the historian, the sources; but considering this here would take us too far.)

Despite the strange, probably psychologically quite revealing aversion to the old formula "to hold to be true" (*für-wahr-halten*), we cannot do without the *factual* content of this: to hold something to be *true*—true, not beautiful, useful, ideal, interesting; and to *hold* something to be true, that is, to make it one's own with the mustering of one's whole being; and both *on the testimony of someone else.* Not based on my perception, not from private deduction, but trusting in the witness and the authority of someone else, whether I understand it or not, often against my own intellectual inclinations, desires, dispositions, which must submit and conform themselves to, and align themselves with the Someone Else, the Stranger.[7]

And in a sermon, Newman said, "Now is it not strange that persons who act in this way, who skip over things in Scripture, and go by their prejudices, and by the bad teaching they have received in Scripture, should yet boast that they are scriptural and go by Scripture, and use their private judgement? No, they do not judge, they do not examine, they do not go by Scripture; but they take just so much of Scripture as suits them, and leave the rest. They go, not by their private judgement, but their private prejudice, and by their private liking." John Henry Newman, "Sermon 4. Prejudice and Faith," in *Faith and Prejudice and Other Unpublished Sermons*, ed. The Birmingham Oratory (New York: Sheed and Ward, 1956), 57–58.

[7] Görres elaborates on this approach to describing belief in chapter 3, "Why We Believe", of Görres, *The Church in the Flesh*, 53–105.

All theology arose from this process, from the endless grappling of many private opinions, views, and attempts at explanation with what was presented, which we call Revelation. Only he who participates in this thinking of the *Church* and also does it himself is a theologian—not someone just using it as a sports field for tossing around his own pet ideas and theories. Otherwise, he will never perceive more than individual tenets and their historical development, individual schools of thought and systems, a disjointed heap without persuasive power, tossed together superficially and haphazardly: you have the parts in your hand; unfortunately, the living band to bind them is missing.[8]

The faith of the theologian is the faith of the Church. Above all, it needs *sentire cum Ecclesia* (to think and to feel with the Church)—the synthesizing sense—which, as a relation to the whole, alone can resist the powerful pull of fragmentation. The living band is the Church herself, which is also the object of our faith and investigation.

For she is the great and, in a certain sense, the only subject of faith, just as she is the actual subject of theology as a community of thought, which includes not only individuals but many generations from many centuries and us as well, as the foliage of one summer.

The Church—always considered as the whole from the first Advent of the Lord until His Return—is the perpetual contemporary of Jesus Christ, always in conversation with Him; she is the object of that promise: the "Spirit, whom [I] will send . . . will teach you all [truth], and bring to your remembrance all that I have said to you."[9] The Church is

[8] Görres is paraphrasing Goethe's *Faust*: "For then he has the separate parts in hand. Too bad! the spirits bond is missing." Johann Wolfgang Goethe, *Faust: First Part / Faust: Erster Teil*, trans. Peter Salm (New York: Bantam, 1962), 119.

[9] Jn 14:26.

the one addressed by the Word; she is the listener par excellence, who, throughout her historical existence, preserves and moves the received Word in her heart; she "develops" it in a darkroom and interprets it; and in her children, she existentially displays it in an incalculable abundance of living "duplicates".[10]

She is present not only horizontally and geographically—as, unfortunately, so many people construe her, in a dubious abridgment—but always, at the same time, vertically and historically. As a contemporary of Christ, she has an enormous memory, which includes not only concepts, ideas, systems, words, and images but also the crystallizations of these in institutions, actions, forms, and customs. We call the content of this "Tradition", the process as well as the material. From this, all of Christianity on earth subsists, including what has been split off and, in addition, a great deal that is extra-Christian, post-Christian.

Have you ever considered the role of memory in our everyday lives? It is only from memory that we live in relation to things and people. Without memory—that is, without recognition—there would be no human community. Without memory, there would be no language—that is, no communication. There is a disorder of certain brain cells called aphasia, in which memory of words fails. I hear everything, acoustically, but sound follows sound without meaning. Only when the memory functions again does the noise become word, speech, context. Anyone who wakes up from anesthesia notices this. At first, he perceives nothing but individual phenomena without meaning, oppressively so without meaning, until the memory catches up: "This is the wall; this the window; this the bed I am lying in." Without

[10] See chapter 1, "Our Image of Christ", for a more detailed version of this analogy to developing and duplicating an image in a darkroom, p. 55, n. 12.

memory, we would simply starve; for we would not be able to identify food as such.

Very similar, frighteningly similar, is the situation with the great memory of the Church as the realm and organ of how things relate. Everything—all talk about God and Christ, all understanding of the Bible—derives its full meaning from this alone, and every further development of understanding, which, of course, still has great possibilities, must allow itself to be fit into this. Again and again, the image of aphasia comes to mind when I see how certain theological tendencies speak today as if there were no valid image of Christ at all, as if no one knew yet who He really was; as if that was just waiting to be discovered; as if, until now, no one had "really" understood the meaning of the words in the Bible (for example, "this is my body")[11] as if we had to start fresh everywhere from nothing in the situation of Robinson (Defoe's hero, not John A. T. Robinson!). Whoever really accepts this simply proves that he is already outside the Church's realm of memory.

What Möhler wrote regarding Church history applies equally well to other areas of faith:

> For if one wants to study the history of the Christian Church successfully and penetrate into the essence of her, it is necessary to bring along a Christian and ecclesiastical sense and spirit. The Christian spirit must have been tested in us, showing some success; we must at least have a receptive sense of it if we want to understand its workings. Otherwise, everything remains a completely impassable territory for us, and it is purely external matters, only the most external relationships that we are able to grasp, and even these we will be able to grasp only in a very skewed and distorted way. . . . It is the [Christian] spirit that works, and since it works in its own way and expresses itself in

[11] Mt 26:26; Lk 22:19.

> these phenomena, one must be familiar with this peculiar spirit in order to find one's way in these phenomena.[12]

That, without this sense, one "perceives only a wild churning of passion, delusion, and impudence in the course of the Christian centuries" is, therefore, quite self-evident; for "one did not know how to penetrate into that which lies deep, precisely because the sense for it is missing."[13]

Only this "sense"[14] allows us to penetrate the innumerable outer shells in which not only history but the entire visible phenomenon of the Church ceaselessly and necessarily develops and enmeshes the Divine at the same time and, in the double sense of the word, "betrays" it.

"There are utterances, representations, revelations of the Christian spirit, in the midst of which we must be situated if what develops out of it is to be understood and properly judged by us."[15]

Theology is the *reflection* on this memory. It is only within these dimensions that it ceases to be mere professorial bickering and a battlefield of opinions and that it corresponds to the magnificent image that Hugo Ball rediscovered from the heritage of the Eastern church in his book *Byzantine Christianity*: "Theology is the meeting place of all endeavors that make existence worth living. It is the heart of peoples and the innermost marrow of their vitality. It is the last line of defense on which great destinies are decided."[16]

That is why the theologian is always only the servant

[12] Johann Adam Möhler, *Kirche und Geschichte*, ed. Bernhard Hanssler (Freiburg im Breisgau: Herder, 1941), 48–49.

[13] Möhler, *Kirche und Geschichte*, 49.

[14] Möhler, *Kirche und Geschichte*, 49–50.

[15] Möhler, *Kirche und Geschichte*, 50.

[16] Hugo Ball, *Byzantinisches Christentum: Drei Heiligenleben (zu Joannes Klimax, Dionysius Areopagita und Symeon dem Styliten)* (1923; Einsiedeln, Switzerland: Benziger Verlag, 1958), 159.

and guardian, messenger and mediator of this treasure, not its master, and he does not control it. He is always just a mere *co*-worker in the purification and development that will be necessary as long as we see only in shadows and mirrors.[17] He never speaks on his own behalf but is rather commissioned by the whole. This is the thing: what distinguishes the theologian from the religious writer is that the theologian speaks in the ministerial office and from this office, which is more than just a civic teaching assignment, no matter how serious and knowledgeable a religious writer may be—even if the latter has completed specialized studies. Kierkegaard, a "learned" theologian, agonized about this over and over again—for the *authority* to express himself religiously. The Church alone is authorized, and she delegates this task through the ministerial office.

Even the prophet who has to proclaim a new partial inspiration, a partial inspiration not yet recognized or forgotten by theology, stands *under* the Church and not beside or above her. The theologian has to measure the prophetic message as to whether and to what extent it can be integrated into the entire *depositum fidei* (deposit of faith). This may often seem downright scandalous to spectators—paradoxical, in any case. Teilhard de Chardin is the most powerful, the most poignant example of such a scrutiny in our day. The prophet may have a religious talent a hundred times stronger than the theologian—that does not matter. But he has received only *one* light, *his* light, for the salvation of the whole, and he must pass it on; and this necessarily one-sided vision must be "held" within the whole.[18] But the whole

[17] See 1 Cor 13:12.

[18] By "held" I understand Görres to mean both contained within as well as lifted off the ground, so to say, and thereby protected. In an essay she wrote in 1956, she uses the same terminology to discuss marriage and the way it is sustained by being a part of a whole and by being protected; she uses the

is never something manifested personally, an individually and spontaneously illuminating "experience" within every piece of the whole. It can only be embraced implicitly and explicated piecemeal. But only the unity of the Church can judge the extent to which private inspiration conforms to or contradicts the whole of Revelation. The great mystics, the saints—they have always known this. The theologian as well as the visionary, like the humblest Christian, only participates in something greater than they can generate or ever comprehend. Again, Möhler:

> This is the mystery of our knowledge of God: only in the whole can he who created the whole be known because he reveals himself completely only in the whole. How is the single individual to know him? Only because the individual, although not the whole, can yet embrace it with great mind, with love. Thus, although *the individual is not the whole*, the whole is yet in the individual and the individual knows what the whole is. We, as individual essences, expand ourselves to the whole in love. . . . To set oneself above one's position in pride is to set aside the whole [to prune it according to our own standard]; we do not thus lift ourselves to the All, but narrow-heartedly draw it down to us and see of God only as much as we are, the many parts of the whole. Although we thus wish to be the whole, we know only what a part knows.[19]

From these related factors, it is self-evident why the theologian needs, as a special requirement of his profession,

---

analogy of the way a nut is protected inside a shell and held off the ground by the tree. See Ida Friederike Görres, "Geleitwort" in Thomas Gilby, *Kleiner Kompaß für Eheleute*, trans. Elisabeth Maurer (Freiburg im Breisgau, Germany: Herder, 1956), 7.

[19] Johann Adam Möhler, *Unity in the Church; or, The Principle of Catholicism: Presented in the Spirit of the Church Fathers of the First Three Centuries*, trans. Peter C. Erb (Washington, D.C.: Catholic University of America Press, 2016), 153, emphasis added by Görres.

humility—namely, that ability and willingness to acknowledge something altogether higher than oneself, and to do so "with a great heart", willingly, joyfully, grateful that it exists and that [this person thinks,] "I *may* serve It and partake of It"; it is the antithesis, then, of that narrow envy, for which every form of superiority is a thorn and a torment, which can be alleviated quickly, time and again, only by the greatest possible criticism and disparagement of that which is higher.

The main antagonist to such humility seems to me to be not even pride but *vanity*. After all, pride can be transformed into the noble pride of [Saint] Christopher, to be the servant of the greatest Lord. But vanity: the addiction to emphasizing constantly one's own beloved self, to present oneself, to attract attention, to be talked about, to be disputed. Luther's harsh statement about reason being a whore also applies very precisely to this situation: vain and venal, ripe for corruptibility, ready to rationalize every useful error and provide the best reasons and proofs for it, if only some increase in prestige beckons as a reward—through being a sensation, through contact with celebrities, through creating a bit of a stir, through attracting a following from young people or certain circles. It would be a psychologically very appealing and rewarding study (if it were possible, and obviously it is not) to analyze the role of vanity in the innumerable divisions of the Church, in the emergence and development of heretical groups.

As unpopular, even taboo, as the word is today, *chastity*—the striving for purity of heart and body—accompanies humility, not only for the sake of the preparation for the priesthood but also for the laity. Chastity is one of the instruments, so to speak, for thinking *about God*. The fact that the organ of spiritual knowledge is clouded and dulled by the indulgence of the instincts is ancient empirical knowledge. That wisdom cannot dwell in an unclean person is already stated in the Old Testament.[20] And if we certainly cannot confine [characterization of] the pure heart—that God can see—to chastity alone, neither can we exclude chastity from it.

Among the hallmarks of the Holy Spirit—whom the theologian must beseech in particular—chastity and abstinence are enumerated just as clearly and emphatically as love, peace, and joy; unchastity in many forms is just as explicit among the contraindications for His presence as are quarrels, discord, and hatred.[21] And whoever wants to teach the people of God in the directives of God, in His will and His way, must at least prove himself to be compliant and obedient to these instructions in his own life, as one who is "exemplary", and not as a ridiculous mini Christian who is always wrangling for his private satisfactions and little pleasures. Anyone who wants to bring tidings of God—may he want to do so in any way other than existentially? And is not the purity of the whole human being an indispensable part of this?

Certainly it is well known that erotic feeling very often increases, even sometimes opens up, religious *feeling*—no wonder, since both are deeply related, in cracking open a certain stratum of imagination, and yet we also know that a knack for the erotic is not even *love* already, nor does it guarantee it; in fact, by keeping love provisional, suggestive, external, it can even make it more difficult for love to come about, to mature. In a very similar relationship, a religious knack does not, by a long shot, mean piety; and focusing on

[20] "Wisdom will not enter a deceitful soul, nor dwell in a body enslaved to sin." Wis 1:4.

[21] For example, see Gal 5:16–26; Eph 5:3–18.

the intellectual or emotional enjoyment of religious content may even complicate the growth of genuine piety, which is essentially obedient love of God. The religious "experience", like the erotic one, must be constantly subject to monitoring, scrutiny, and purification. As for what has happened in religious "experience" in its untamed state, very often mixed up wickedly with disguised or open eroticism—Church history knows enough about this.

As the last element of that basic attitude that we called piety and that blossoms in humility and purity, we also mention love *for the listener*, love for the unlearned, the simple, the "ordinary Christians", who, unfortunately, so often appear to the learned theologians only as a disdained object to be taught and "enlightened". Are they not to be understood as the "poor of Christ" just as much as the materially poor? And is not the saying still valid today that the Father reveals to little ones what He hides from the clever ones? What might the strict theological knowledge of Benedict or Francis of Assisi or Thérèse of Lisieux have looked like? And how is it with the innumerable "little ones" who live according to their catechism and the Gospel and the Schott Missal and perhaps some diluted rule of the great [saints]? Even a thimble filled to the brim is still full. It is better to help them to reach such fullness in their own language than to baffle and confuse them and tug at their roots with an accoutrement of unintelligible foreign words. C. S. Lewis, as so often, hits the nail on the head when he writes to a friend (in the face of an element of addiction to liturgical experimentation, even among Anglicans!): ultimately, "the charge to Peter was Feed my sheep; not Try experiments on my rats, or even, Teach my performing dogs new tricks"![22]

[22] C. S. Lewis, *Letters to Malcolm: Chiefly on Prayer* (New York: Harcourt, Brace and World, 1964), 5.

But these last questions are more relevant to theologians who have finished their studies than to those still studying, although even the latter like to appear as reformers of the stupid churchgoers, to whom they would like to impart their own latest ideas as soon as possible. The beginner, like every beginner, must learn this first: to practice the form of prudence called *docilitas* (gentleness or teachability). After all, someone who wants to learn must *trust* the teacher. This is probably a seriously neuralgic spot in the study of theology today. Whom should the one who wants to learn trust? All the views are thrust upon him at the same time—those that preserve as well as those that tear down. Here, it seems to me, that compass we spoke of at the beginning comes into play in a meaningful way. He can really only trust the Holy Spirit and the Church. And Holy Scripture gives us certain features, it seems to me. The beginner cannot choose his teachers, and, humanly, he has little justification to judge them. At least he can get an impression and examine for himself whether the teacher *even speaks out of "reverence syndrome"* and whether he wants to address the "reverence syndrome" in the listener, to awaken it, nourish it, and educate it—or the opposite. "Never sit on the bench of the mockers, they are lowest of men", wrote Matthias Claudius to his son.[23] "It is so easy to break eggs without making omelettes", says Lewis again.[24]

Finally—to conclude these rather fragmentary reflections:

[23] Görres paraphrases Claudius, who writes, "Do not sit where the scoffers sit, for they are the most wretched of all creatures!" Perhaps Görres had the whole passage in mind. Claudius continues, "Respect not the sanctimonious but the pious people and follow them! A man who has true fear of God in his heart is like the sun that shines and warms, even when it does not speak" (translation by Bryson). Matthias Claudius, "An seinen Sohn", in *The Oxford Book of German Prose / Das Oxforder Buch Deutscher Prosa: Von Luther bis Rilke*, ed. H. G. Fiedler (Oxford, U.K.: Oxford University Press, 1943), 123.

[24] Lewis, *Letters to Malcolm*, 6.

Regarding the very old custom, which has persisted to our time, of granting theology studies only to those who commit themselves to the lifelong *exclusive service of God* in the Church as consecrated persons, there are some good reasons for this. Even if it has been abolished as a principle today, its root still exists as a question, as a very serious question—namely, whether those who direct their spiritual energies full-time for years to the knowledge and proclamation of God should not "ultimately" also be awakened and drawn to the love of God, even to passion for God, as the purpose of life. There is already more than an external connection, explained only historically, only sociologically, between theology and the priesthood, no matter how much the catechist has his own reasons for his life. Theology as a mere minor field of study seems to me to be a phenomenon that is strange and difficult to understand.

"Theology ceases to be what theology means when it places itself in line with history, philology, and psychology. And it thus loses any meaning at all." So wrote Guardini in his highly thought-provoking essay on "Anselm [of Canterbury] and the Nature of Theology" in his unjustly forgotten collection *Auf dem Wege* (*On the Way*).[25]

Since today, however, access is open to every Tom, Dick, and Harry, for whatever motives students choose this subject, one can only hope that, within this development, the different, still indistinctly intertwined groups will gradually separate from each other: the mere students of religion who seek only information and nothing more; the others, who are the *intellectus quaerens fidem* (understanding seeking faith)—who seek an orientation for themselves in theology;

[25] Romano Guardini, "Anselm von Canterbury und das Wesen der Theologie", in *Auf dem Wege* (Mainz: Matthias-Grünewald-Verlag, 1923), 53.

the actual theologians who embody the *fides quaerens intellectum* (faith seeking understanding); those called to be catechists—for whom one wonders, however, whether a distinct training designed for their special task would not be much more appropriate and something important, rather than the detour via the conventional program of studies required for the priesthood.

And finally, one can wish just one thing for the young people who choose this course of study for sincere and good reasons, even if the ultimate implications are still unclear: that they would venture so close to the fire that one day it seizes and devours them, that at least a few (there have never been many) are swept away from increased *knowledge* of God into *passion* for God, which will then claim their whole person, their whole destiny. May they, roused out of the laudable "minor in religion", either choose the priesthood or form a new state of full-time catechists who go out where they are *really* needed, behind iron and other curtains, to Latin America, to those places where proclamation requires a "boldness" different from that for which people are lauded today, who amuse themselves in the completely safe sport of challenging helpless authorities—where proclamation really still means existential commitment and bearing ultimate witness to Christ.

Theology in itself cannot yield the charisma of the Apostles or even the gifts of "sacred science" and the interpretation of Scripture. It can even hinder them severely; but it can also open a door to them. It *can* point to the Fire, in the direction of the Fire: may the Fire burn Its way over to us and transform people into being Its rays on earth, as the Lord desired that It should blaze.

5

Remarks on Celibacy

I

For some years now, celibacy, once extolled as a high privilege and distinguishing mark of the Latin priesthood, has been presented with increasing insistence, and nowadays with bitter passion, as one of the most serious obstacles on the path to a priestly vocation, as if it were an alien element in our image of the priest, hauled in long ago by an unworldly aversion to life, then forcefully fastened on to the office. Even if—despite its suspicious, nonbiblical origins—it has a certain lofty (or exaggerated) idealism that cannot be denied, still, experience has simply shown that monastic ideology does not stand up to life as it is. Thus, in many respects, celibacy has proven more harmful than beneficial, both to the individual and to the Church. It is no wonder that many young men who in themselves are inclined to serving at the altar and to pastoral care shy away from this incomprehensible burden. In view of the increasing concern about the necessary number of priests, it is therefore a serious concern that our era, committed to reform, should also freely consider whether such a meaningless and burdensome remnant out of centuries different from ours would not be better abolished.

Confronted with this endlessly and ever more vehemently repeated polemic, we must first ask about the idea lying at the root of such objections. It results mostly in a purely negative image of celibacy and those who are celibate. Here, what embeds itself in the awareness of many believers is a figure of pure negation composed of many more or less clear impressions and prejudices, unsifted and unclarified. For example: the celibate priest is basically a poor wretch who could do better. He is forbidden that which he, like every other human being, secretly desires the most—namely, full and legitimate erotic-sexual satisfaction, whether it is understood more physically or bodily as well as mentally at the same time; it is something that most people value as so central, so indispensable, that an existence that lacks this simply appears to them as "not a life". But the priest is also deprived of the most precious emotional goods, of family life, of his own children, of a sheltering home. Moreover, everyone knows how much what is forbidden tantalizes and mesmerizes. It can therefore be assumed that the priest is not less but more occupied with these things in his imagination, in his desires, than many laymen, perhaps also constantly in search of substitutes—some harmless, some less so. He will probably often have something to hide that does not correspond to his way of life, and if he does not have that, he will often have to wither away in heart and mind. This, then, results in those rough, hardened types who, by commanding and coldly asserting their authority, feel they have to emphasize the security that is not afforded them by the affirmation of love. In addition, "they do not know life"—how *could* someone who is excluded from its most intense experiences? Nevertheless, it is precisely in these matters that he claims to have a say and make the rules: "They impose heavy burdens on others and do not lift a finger themselves!"[1]

[1] See Mt 23:4.

This state of affairs cannot be beneficial or useful to the priest himself or to the people of the Church—so it is high time to abolish it.

Those who speak in this way usually cannot imagine any other reason for a prohibition than that the object of the prohibition is bad and dangerous: so, they conclude, the priest, even if he tells us otherwise, must still find marriage and a love life fundamentally evil, base, and sinful. But these are dark medieval prejudices ("taboos", as they are called in the illustrated magazines with an educated veneer), in which no one believes today and which, therefore, should no longer form the basis for a law of the Church. And when some advocates of celibacy respond that the priest, in this way, needs to save time and energy for the service of the Church, this convinces the critics only slightly. For, they say, today most laypeople lead such an intense, even frenzied, working life that quite a few priests could take this as a model. And not only is this not hindered by family life, but this would not even be possible for most men if they did not encounter in family life a fresh source of strength for their professional commitment every day. How little time a man devotes directly to his wife and children! Far too little, in fact—often contributing to the hardship of the wife, often to the detriment of the children, but at least not to the detriment of his career. So what actually prevents the priest from doing the same? Apart from the fact that one does not get the impression that every clergyman—think here of peaceful rural or small-town conditions—is consumed by his duties in the same merciless way as so many laymen are consumed by theirs. Many priests would have enough time and leisure to devote themselves to both areas, as can be seen not only in Protestant pastors but also in doctors and others in charitable professions. And would not many priests be more human and, therefore, more convincing and successful in their profession than when they are lonely, bitter, and dissatisfied and have to look for a substitute for what they have been denied, what they lack?

~

We need to listen to such objections, concerns, even accusations, and deal with them honestly in order to look at the matter from all sides. But it is precisely when we do this with what has been put forward that we are struck by how one-sidedly it starts from a single point of view, namely, a negative one—what they understand of celibacy is only one thing: prohibition and deprivation. But is this the whole thing? Is it the heart of the matter and the purpose of this enterprise?

Is not that as if we wanted to see only the wall in a garden, and only the sweat and sore muscles in sports? Yes, even marriage could, if one wanted, be portrayed in a purely negative way: as a prohibition on getting involved with a third party, a prohibition on divorce if things go wrong, even more so a prohibition on remarrying. But would such a description do justice to marriage? Certainly, the judgments we reproduced above are partly based on actual observations, on widespread facts—but they are chosen one-sidedly: all are examples of failed or poorly managed celibacy. It is truly a tragic and terrible thing—not unlike a failed, poorly handled marriage. But would we want to determine the meaning and nature of marriage from the many broken marriages that we encounter every day?

~

First, the experience of a healthy, happy marriage and a healthy, happy priestly life is relevant. We must observe and listen to this and draw our conclusions from it. It is a misjudgment to think that a renunciation could only be forced or only based on the rejection of the object. Or does a man choose a young lady because he thinks all other young ladies are ugly or wicked? No, rather because he likes her better! And is he sad about the others whom he is forced to "renounce" by such a choice? Does a young lady accept a man only because she hates her childhood home? Even if she departs with tears and heartache, she gladly and voluntarily follows the one she loves.

The priest is not forced into a heartless, emotionally void existence; he is not banished to the desert; rather, he chooses a different community of life and love: with Christ and with the Church. Celibacy is only the gateway to and the boundary line to this. It is an offer, an opportunity—just like marriage. One can make great, glorious things out of both; one can fail at both.

The priest "sacrifices" the joys and blessings of human love and marriage. Does this mean that he despises them? In all religions of all peoples, people have always sacrificed what is precious, not what is bad and shabby; the latter would be an insult to the deity. Nor did the ancient forms of pagan sacrifice have the purpose of destroying the offering: it was to be elevated—the slaughtered animal to be the food of the gods, the burned fruit transformed into the sacred flame, the sign and image of divine existence. In the Christian sacrifice of the altar, as well, bread and wine are transformed, elevated beyond their nature.

This is also the case in this context.

~

It would be far too narrow and superficial to regard the "undivided ministry" of the priest as a mathematical question of hours and managing tasks. We have to look at the whole of this. Those who argue that the priest could just as well "perform" his "ministerial functions" as a married man have clearly not yet grasped the true connection between family and professional life. A man "belongs" to his family not only in the hours of immediate togetherness, after work (where there still is such a thing), or on vacation. Already his years as a young man are largely, often mainly, filled with the search for a lifelong companion, with the many social encounters and acquaintances that ultimately serve this choice; then with getting to know each other, courting, cherishing each other, planning together, and establishing a home, be it even the smallest apartment. How much his imagination, his conversations, his striving revolve around this future! And also later, even if his family members seem rightly to sigh at how little they have of him: what is behind the energy, the zeal with which he concentrates on his work—it is his will and aspiration, which are, after all, to establish himself in, preserve, enlarge, and enhance his family's living space; to appear in the eyes of his wife as the one who keeps what he has promised and what she expects of him. Even if he does not "think about it" explicitly, this intention is like a person's lifeblood, the sap that permeates the tree down to the individual tips of the branches, to each leaf.

It is good and right that it is so. We must not underestimate the power, might, and dignity of this driving force, which really is what has transformed and continues to transform the face of our earth. And this urge also grows out of the old mysterious root, the dark one, which we call, with a most inadequate phrase, "generative power".[2] It is just as much a part of this as the biological processes that people make so much, far too much, of a fuss about. We must not limit them so narrowly, so severely. Thus, the wise and pious Lutheran theologian Hans Asmussen tells us about parenthood in his little book, which cannot be recommended enough, *Das Geheimnis der Liebe* (*The Secret of Love*) (only sixty-four pages, but how precious they are!):

> What is this "drive to reproduce"? Humans and animals have it in common. Is it really the same in humans and animals? I deny that. Only degenerate people can believe that. . . . It is impossible to look for the will to have a child only in the physical being of humans. . . . As love urges us to step out of ourselves so that we may unite with another human for life, so that force that we mistakenly call "sex drive" and is actually our deepest self, also means this: that we step out of ourselves, break through the barriers of our ego in order to become "more", greater, and more comprehensive than we are on our own. Words are not enough to express what our deepest self actually anticipates from having children.[3]

[2] The word I translate as "generative power" (*Geschlechtskraft*) could also be translated as "the power of sex". I opted for "generative power" because of the way Görres uses the term *Geschlecht* in near-contemporary works. "Generative power" should be understood both in terms of *generations* within kinship and the *generation* of new life through reproduction. In other works, Görres uses *Geschlecht* (and sometimes the Latin term *gens* instead) to communicate both related senses of the term. See Ida Friederike Görres, *Be-Denkliches: Über die Mischehe und anderes Zeitgespräch* (Donauwörth, Germany: Verlag Ludwig Auer, 1966); *What Binds Marriage Forever*, trans. Jennifer S. Bryson (Washington, D.C.: Catholic University of America Press, 2025).

[3] Hans Asmussen, *Das Geheimnis der Liebe* (Stuttgart: Evangelisches Verlagswerk, 1962), 53–54. The terms I translate as "drive to reproduce" and "sex drive" are *Fortpflanzungstrieb* and *Geschlechtstrieb*, respectively.

As for this deepest self and its power: they should not be extinguished and choked off in celibacy—that would truly mean doing damage that can no longer be made up for and also cannot be justified. No, that central force, the living response in us to the first of all God's commands—"Be fruitful and multiply!"[4]—is what is raised up, transformed, in the sacrifice. That humans "break through the barriers of our ego in order to become 'more', greater, and more comprehensive than we are on our own":[5] word for word, this formulation is correct. The priest should step into, grow into, the destiny of Christ, who, as a man who was a virgin, sacrificed His entire mighty power to awaken and to form in order to transform all mankind as a body in the Kingdom of God, to multiply and increase the fellowship of His love on earth at all times. Christ, the "Man of the Church": the priest should "re-present" Him also in this—visibly, clearly, recognizably.

Certainly, sacrifice means something deep, incisive, "getting serious". Everything precious comes at a great cost. Just as, with a grapevine, all the shoots are cut back except for the one into which all growth and the power to bear fruit are to be concentrated and consolidated, so too here. Just as, in a valley that is to become a reservoir, all the verdant life on the slopes and at the bottom is relentlessly buried under the flood, so that this depth becomes a source of power, light, and life in a wide area, so too here. We know that all our technology is based on "conversion of energy", in differ-

[4] Gen 1:28.

[5] Asmussen, Das Geheimnis der Liebe, 54.

ent ways. We are familiar with the locomotive that converts coal into steam, the car that converts gasoline into speed, the turbine generators of the overland lines, in which the power in water is "transformed"—that is, recast—into a current. Thus, celibacy should become a powerful transformer that reconfigures the natural power to blossom and procreate so that it flows to many people as an overabundance of eternal life of grace.

In a certain sense, the priest "dies" from it, because he renounces the physical heirs who actualize a person's earthly continued existence; but he dies voluntarily and literally "for the people", out of that love of which the Lord says there is none greater than in the one who lays down his life "for the brethren".[6] But precisely in this he becomes, in a new and special way, one of the "sons of the resurrection",[7] as the Gospel calls those who, for the sake of the Kingdom of Heaven, have renounced the dignity and delight of bodily procreation and all that belongs to it: for they already mysteriously are an image of that state of coming glory, when we will all, participating in the Resurrection of Christ, on the New Earth, in the New Heaven, be men and women, body and soul, but "neither marry nor [be] given in marriage",[8] because death has been overcome—death, which has continually demanded new physical births.

[6] 1 Jn 3:16.

[7] Lk 20:36. "Sons of the resurrection" is also the title of an essay Görres wrote about celibacy in the priesthood. Ida Friederike Görres, "Section I: Sons of the Resurrection," in *Is Celibacy Outdated?*, trans. Barbara Waldstein-Wartenberg (Westminster, Md.: Newman Press, 1965), 6–55.

[8] Mt 22:30.

Of course, the establishment of celibacy does not in itself bring about this transformation, any more than the "I do" of marriage brings about the transformation of drive and passion into the irrevocable fusion of hearts. Both must be striven for and borne with suffering throughout life. The priest who has correctly understood celibacy is only he who, with all his heart and with entirely free consent, faces and wants to persevere in this painful, auspicious transformation and reorientation of his whole being and life. He who recognizes that he is so overcome by God and committed to serve Him will certainly not become a comfortable "bourgeois man with spirituality" who "manages his tasks" and at the same time devotes himself leisurely to himself. The man who is overcome in this way is not "single" and thus "free of" burdens and cares but, rather, is deeply bound like his Lord, whose fare to eat was to do the will of the Father, and, like Him, he bears the burdens of all his brothers.[9] From being a merely unwed man, he becomes, in this way, a virgin. How much this word in the minds of people today has been turned into kitsch and hollowed out! Only sometimes does its real meaning still reach us—for exam-

[9] See Jn 4:34; Ps 68:19; Gal 6:2. In German, Görres packs nuance into this sentence. First, my use of "single" and "free of" together translate one German word: *ledig*, which has both meanings. In modern German, the word *ledig* is used almost exclusively to mean "single" or "unwed". However, the meaning of *ledig* in the sense of "single" or "unwed" derives etymologically from the root meaning of *ledig*—namely, "to be free of", which, in turn, derives from *gelenkig*, meaning "agile, flexible". Görres, with nuance, implies both meanings here. Second, the phrase "fare to eat" translates *Speise*. *Speise* means not just food in a generic sense but, rather, a dish served at a meal; in this way, Görres is communicating that, for the priest, giving of himself for others by doing the will of the Lord reflects the way Christ gave of Himself for others in doing the will of the Father. And the image of food served *as a meal* is, of course, bursting with eucharistic resonance.

ple, when one speaks of a virgin field or, as in some languages, a virgin forest, that is, a primeval forest; this means untouched, unexploited, offering the cumulative fullness of its original vigor. And there is one more thing: it is true that, just as one reviles only a stronger enemy, for a long time Christianity feared the power of sex too much and, out of fear and self-defense, disparaged and reviled it too much for a complicated bundle of reasons that we cannot even begin to delineate here. Therefore, it is right and proper that we should strive today to rediscover, understand anew, and praise sex as a glorious gift from God. But we always tend to throw the baby out with the bathwater and throw out the tub afterward. That is, today one forgets only too easily that the old warnings and severe judgments were not just exaggerations and prejudices but that they rested on a broad foundation of very sober and deep experience and knowledge of life and that this core must be retained if we want to become and remain Christians. The actual life of the sexes on this earth needs redemption; otherwise, it becomes corrupt, spoils, and rots in a terrible way. Its redemption manifests itself in the holy attitude of chastity, which expresses itself partly in marriage, in love full of fruitful surrender, and partly in renunciation, in the obligatory renunciation under the commandment, and in the voluntary renunciation of vows and obedience to celibacy. If, in the past, we often made sex the devil, today it is often made an idol that dominates human life with near omnipotence. That is why the one who renounces, whether he knows it or not, is also a lofty flag of resistance to a mass madness, a testimony to the freedom of man against a superstition (no matter how it may camouflage itself as "scientific" or "academic") that claims and believes that no man could live healthily and happily without what the ancients coarsely and plainly called "the lust of the flesh".

~

It need not be true that such a man "knows nothing of life". Certainly, in some things he remains "a stranger and a pilgrim",[10] but he who wanders on the heights often sees more of the country than he who is in the midst of the hustle and bustle. And brotherly empathy can be more enlightened and enlightening than the selfish gathering of experiences. In addition, deprivation is often a genuine way of knowing: *per exclusionem*, by excluding. That sounds contradictory, but do not orphans often know more deeply and keenly what parents are, those who are childless what a gift children are, a sick person what health is, a refugee or exile what home means? Many things become clearer at a distance than in the midst of a scrum. In this context, the different modes of experience of priests and laypeople must be discussed and thought through honestly with each other, for the good of both.

~

We all know of solitary trees in the landscape, trees of striking size and beauty: the beech tree, the linden tree on the hill, looms visibly from afar—a signpost for hikers, providing shade in the heat and protection from the rain for all who come. They have always struck me as images of those generous, solitary ones consecrated to God and given to mankind.

[10] See Eph 2:19.

II

In 1831, the archbishop of Freiburg refused to allow a number of graduates to be ordained to the priesthood because they had sent to the seat of government in Baden a statement of approval for a petition to abolish celibacy by state law.[11] The seminarians then sought to make amends, with the apology that "they had been *taught* theoretical objections to the celibacy law *for years*"—namely, by their instructors. Three professors of the faculty of theology publicly fought celibacy and religious orders. The great Möhler, their colleague in Tübingen, passed judgment on one of them: "Whoever listens to his lectures could only be filled with a boundless contempt for Christianity." So, nothing new under the sun!

[11] From the late 1820s to the mid-1830s, several Catholic theology professors at the University of Freiburg, enthusiasts of the Enlightenment, were pushing to abolish the requirement of clerical celibacy. Other reforms they urged included a liturgy in German, revising the missal, and curtailing pilgrimages. Freiburg was likely one of the targets of Pope Gregory XVI's condemnation of "the abominable conspiracy against clerical celibacy" in his encyclical *Mirari vos* in 1832 (no. 11).

In a Swedish translation of an excerpt from this chapter, published a year after this book, the date is 1832, not 1831. Ida Görres, "Från celibat till äktenskap?", *Credo* 51, no. 1 (1971), 9. By contrast, in an excerpt of this essays published in a newspaper in 1969, the date is 1828. Ida Friederike Görres, "Überbetonung des Maskulinen drängt in der Kirche Flucht vor der 'Mutter' Kirche", *Die Furche*, August 9, 1969, 9. The controversy in Freiburg was ongoing in 1828, 1831, and 1832. However, 1831 appears to be the correct date for the particular incident to which Görres refers. Karl-Heinz Braun, "'Seine Zelibatspolemik wird ihm keine Rosen bringen': Zum Freiburger Moraltheologen Heinrich Schreiber und seinen Kollegen in der Theologischen Fakultät", *Zeitschrift des Breisgau-Geschichtsvereins Schau-ins-Land*, no. 116 (1997), 215. Special thanks to Alkuin Schachenmayr, O.Cist., for assistance with this citation.

This happened in the late days of the Enlightenment and in the early stages of the revolutions of [18]48. In the hundred years that followed, it seems that celibacy was accepted within the Church—although the attacks from Protestants, liberals, Kulturkampf fighters,[12] and freethinkers never ceased! It was simply accepted as an unalterable fact and defended in its entirety, like every other Catholic issue. When under attack, one rallies around what is threatened without examining it further for value and worthiness. The questioning of celibacy arose only later, not under external pressure, not even as a protest; it was open and trusting, out of a desire for clarification and insight, in the circles of the Youth Movement, the early Liturgical Movement, and among others carrying out the Catholic renewal after World War I. It was not celibacy that was questioned, but the conventional, mostly purely negative *justification* of it out of a devaluation of marriage, woman, sex, eros, nature. The conversation did not stand in isolation but was part of a great awakening that aimed at the religious, the Christian *rehabilitation of nature* (a word that is taboo again today, but under different auspices!), as the good and beloved Creation of God, distinguished from the "evil world". A believing, pious "return to nature" accomplished the long-overdue retrieval of suspect and reviled values. Thus, in the face of these, celibacy and religious vows had to prove themselves anew. They did so in the sense of a free renunciation of the highest goods in life for the sake of undivided devotion to God and to their brothers. The concept of sacrifice was purified, deepened, elevated.

[12] The Kulturkampf ("civilizational struggle" or "culture war") was a conflict from 1872 to 1887 between the German government under Bismarck and the Catholic Church over the control of schools, Church appointments, and other aspects of Church life.

The *historicity* of celibacy was also clearly expressed at that time, set apart from the practice of the early Church and no longer misunderstood as something timelessly unconditional. But the generation of the middle of the [nineteenth] century did not yet take offense at a process of becoming and growth in the Church. They affirmed historical Tradition as the development of a living organism; they searched it not only for human errors but, even more, for the uninterrupted guidance of the Holy Spirit, in which subjective insight has to extend and to direct itself with docility.

In the current state of the discussion, many of the positive approaches to the debate at that time seem to have intensified strangely into something aggressive and negative. The reevaluation of eros and sex, of marriage and family—with the zeitgeist being added to the mix in various ways—gradually gave rise to an attitude that Dr. Albert Görres, physician, theologian, and psychotherapist, describes as follows:

> Today there is a *Catholic sexual mythology* that relishes referring to so-called modern depth psychology or the so-called results of anthropology, according to which it is said to have been proven that without experiencing sexual intercourse, man cannot reach personal maturity but *must* rather become neurotic. All I can say is that this sentence is the paragon of an unscientific assertion. There is not a single bit of empirical evidence for this, not even a trace. It is an ideological statement based merely on that vague plausibility that is the source of much error. . . . Against this speaks the experience that there are probably at least as many mature men among Catholic priests as there are

among lawyers . . . among teachers and doctors, and among Protestant pastors.[13]

Also, the "revaluation"—almost a rediscovery—of the layman and his natural Christian life in the world, most recently solemnly confirmed and emphasized by the [Second Vatican] Council, is being reworked into a push against celibacy; this is probably in the wake of a wave that is sweeping over our entire earth. Deeply ambivalent, it appears primarily as an *expression of "the global power of envy"*, which relentlessly pushes "from below" for uniformity, for the eradication of all differentiation in distinguishing attributes or status.[14] Secondarily, this is answered "from above" by a great, painful urge for justice as reparation—though it is often actually just a bad conscience that identifies with and submits to those accusations, an anti-injustice that would willingly blur all gradations from above and below in order to abolish objects of envy. A segment of laypeople is suddenly developing a mentality of "being oppressed", full of resentment and demands; a segment of priests, some very good ones, are conceding to them partway—ashamed, confessing, and ready to repent. The Council has made clear enough what is right and meaningful in this dynamic: the full Christian

[13] Albert Görres, "Psychologische Bemerkungen zur Krise eines Berufsstandes", in *Weltpriester nach dem Konzil*, Münchener Akademie-Schriften, vol. 46, ed. Franz Heinrich (Munich: Kösel Verlag, 1969), 132–33. Albert Görres was the brother-in-law of Ida Görres. (Ida Görres has a parenthetical citation in the German edition with partial information about this publication: " 'Weltpriester nach dem Konzil', Sonderdruck der Münchener Akademie-Schriften.")

[14] Related to this, Görres addresses the role of the "global power of *envy*" in fostering "pressure to change Church teaching and practice regarding marriage" in section 10 of the book she wrote in 1971: Ida Friederike Görres, *What Binds Marriage Forever*, trans. Jennifer S. Bryson (Washington, D.C.: Catholic University of America Press, 2025).

vocation of the layman in the People of God, the priestly office as brotherly service. This trend, however, wants—far beyond that—almost to reverse the roles; some priests speak and write as if they now wanted to elevate laymen to become their masters, seeing themselves only as the functionaries and spokesmen of the laity and, thus, basically denying the *essentially indispensable share of the priest in the representation of Christ the Lord in His priestly*, teaching, and pastoral office. They no longer want to acknowledge the special dignity and sublimity of their calling; in a strange mixture of humility, feelings of guilt, and feelings of inferiority, they no longer want to be distinguished from the laity by anything, not by attire, nor by the status of being a "respected person", nor even by *consecration*, which is accordingly devalued. This, of course, also removes any reason for a special way of life that would be appropriate for the priest as someone who is distinguished, indelibly shaped by Christ. The priest would like to blend in with the masses, appear only sporadically to perform a few functions, and submerge again without a trace, to share in every worldly lot: the path to marriage is unobstructed; indeed, it almost has to be taken in order to make the assimilation complete.

Intimately linked to this trend is the theological *devaluation of the Eucharist* into a mere "Lord's Supper" in the Reformed [Protestant] understanding. When Luther condemned the Mass as "idolatry", celibacy soon fell away. There are deeply rooted, unspoken connections here.

~

Perhaps even more powerful is the effect of a third, subliminal tangle of themes: under the banner of the aggiornamento (updating, modernization), but without any substantive connection to this, other than the new freedom of speech, there is a striking *overemphasis on the masculine* in the Church (incidentally, also cheered on and imitated by many women). It is the one-sided exaggeration of a mentality that Karl Stern describes as "Cartesian", as "modern scientism. The naive and dangerous belief in an absolute manageability; the absolutism of the scientific method, with a devaluation of wisdom", which exists out of other sources, "a scotomization of the mystery; the sense of organization taking precedence over the sense of organism".[15] [Is it any] wonder that this mentality dismisses everything that contradicts and resists it as myth, magic, superstition, sentimentality, as infantile and archaic. It represents an amazing flight from the feminine—as the key terms indicate it: a spirit of receiving and preserving, organic growth, silent reverence, intuition. Intimation, sympathy, wisdom. A flight in the world and in the realm of the spirit but, above all, in man himself, from the feminine. This rejection crystallizes and mobilizes in revolt against one of the greatest "feminine" figures in the world: the Church, Mother Church.

Some would like to interpret the crisis of the Catholic priest as part of the much-discussed dismissal, disempowerment, even *abolition of the father*, in insurrection against the paternal authority of the pope and bishops. To me, the symptoms of the *rebellion against the mother* seem even clearer—the mother,

[15] Karl Stern, *The Flight from Woman* (New York: Farrar, Straus and Giroux, 1965), 102.

through whose great image the Church has been understood since early times: as Mother and Virgin, as evidenced by the patristic research of Father Hugo Rahner, S.J. It is strange that the Church, represented externally by the purely male clergy, was always recognized internally for her "feminine" character!

It is precisely this aspect that is being contested today. Out of fear of this, a certain type of priest accepts only the strict "male" elements in her as valid: *Theology*, and this *only* as "scientific" and subject to positivist disciplines such as philology and religious studies. *Law*, despite all the accusations against the existing canon law, it is now essentially about new rights and claims—for example, regarding marriage. In the liturgy: despite some individual successful reforms, there is the pedagogical-propagandistic aspect, rationalization, objectification, reduction of stillness and silence, worship for the sake of speaking and immediate effect, clearing out all the "somber" sections that demand acclimating oneself, waiting, and meditating, the abolition of bodily gestures of reverence, of customs bearing clear meaning, of "images" in a broad sense.

In *Tradition*, the great bone of contention, the "feminine" of the Church is clearly embodied: the "womb" that has received and slowly bears fruit to maturity, the place and element of (now so frowned upon!) interiority, mysticism, symbols, of the forces of growth that can never be completely explained, of the invisible beginnings, the web of roots, the silent confluences and their immense fruitfulness, the history that never justifies itself, the memory of figures and destinies—everything multilayered, multivalued, always adjacent to chaos, absolutely in need of the male judgment of discernment and its guidance, but indispensable material for the world of faith.

All of this should now be cut back as far as possible, replaced by abstractions, structures made out of words, activities with an agenda, ruthlessly implemented isolated principles, with everything being "efficient" and completely transparent. Is the naked skeleton more than the breathing flesh, the bare floor plan of greater value than the inhabited home? In this trend, the reduction in the understanding of the Eucharist as well as the hostility to *Marian veneration* appear as directly logical, and from both flows the devaluation of sacrifice, atonement, chastity, and virginity, all of which are now even gladly condemned as pagan, pre-Christian, merely "religious-historical": because in these things, mystery is revealed in a form that has matured over a long time.

But no one can live amid the reduction of everything purely to understanding and practicality, not even a Christian or a priest. It is no wonder that he seeks the missing feminine element, the banished and suppressed feminine element, as an almost inevitable compensation elsewhere: in eros and marriage, by throwing himself into the arms of the concrete, corporeal woman. This urge is reinforced by the fact that "woman" has always been a symbol of the world and worldliness. The cleric, whose relationship to the world is not in order, as he clearly feels, seeks the "world" he lacks in his own wife.

~

Dogma, says C. G. Jung, is always the result and fruit of many minds and many centuries. The same applies to celibacy, the figure of the priest, and many other realities of

Catholic life. Of course, one *cannot* look for them in the *wording of the Gospel*, since they are only part of that "bread" that rose from the long-fermenting effect of the "yeast" in the "three measures of flour".[16] It is strange that the attackers fail to grasp this simple fact of development, while they talk otherwise incessantly about progress and evolution!

The *law of celibacy* is an institution; the fulfilled life of the virgin priest is a *mystery*. Is the charism to be pitted against forced-coupling with the law? That this is usually not an invading imposition but, rather, an answer to fervent, persistent prayer and struggle—it is precisely this gift of grace that Tradition knows: "given to those who wish, clamor, ask, strive for it" (John Chrysostom). Millions of destinies quietly confirm this. As for anyone who no longer wants to proclaim chastity within and outside of marriage, even to laypeople, for whom virginity is ideological gibberish—how should he seek it for himself? Can he see anything else in it than being violated and a claim to life that has been denied?

Certainly, today's celibate *way of life* has room for development and is very much in need of it, but in the depths and in the heights and thereby forward, not by sliding backward in capitulation. Teilhard de Chardin wrote a small important study on the "Evolution of Chastity"—from a mere ethical virtue to its full, destined mystical unfolding: not impoverishment and separation but a new way of deeper penetration of the universe, a conquest of new, lively, and fruitful relationships between man and woman, the "second discovery of fire".[17] "Virginity rests upon chastity as thought upon

[16] See Mt 13:33.

[17] Görres is paraphrasing the conclusion of this essay: "The day will come when, after harnessing the ether, the winds, the tides, gravitation, we shall harness for God the energies of love. And, on that day, for the second time

life."[18] Admittedly, this fearless thinker also says, "Once reason has rejected God, man becomes incapable of conceiving the majesty of virginity or even the duty of procreation (in marriage)."[19]

These considerations show that we live in a *miserable climate for celibacy*—but this says nothing at all about the sense or nonsense of it. The climate is also extremely adverse for completely natural and Christian values that are inherited, such as gratitude and reverence, chastity, natural virginity, and the blessing of children; they stand like fields of plants in the midst of a water shortage. It requires above-average mental resistance to the elements—that is, heft of character—

---

in the history of the world, man will have discovered fire." Pierre Teilhard de Chardin, "The Evolution of Chastity", in *Toward the Future*, trans. René Hague (New York: Harcourt Brace Jovanovich, 1975), 86–87.

[18] Chardin, "Evolution of Chastity", 85.

[19] Görres may be paraphrasing the following passage. Teilhard de Chardin writes of "two . . . phases in the creative transformation of human love":

> During a first phase of humanity, man and woman are confined to the physical act of giving and the concern with reproduction; and around that fundamental act they gradually develop a growing nimbus of spiritual exchanges. At first it was no more than an imperceptible fringe, but the fruitfulness and mystery of union gradually find their way into it; and it is on the side of that nimbus that the balance ultimately comes to rest. However, at that very moment, the centre of physical union from which the light emanated is seen to be incapable of accepting further expansion. The centre of attraction suddenly withdraws ahead, to infinity, we might say; and, in order to continue to possess one another more fully in spirit, the lovers are obliged to turn away from the body, and so seek one another in God.

"Evolution of Chastity", 85. In the German text, Görres has a parenthetical note after this passage: "(Henri de Lubac, T.d.Ch. Hymne an das Ewig-Weibliche, deutsch von H.U.v. Balthasar, Einsiedeln 1968)".

not to be dragged along by the gigantic steamroller of public opinion. As we know, however, in Catholic education in particular, the virtues required for this were scarcely cultivated consciously because the "embedded" person was supported by many other forces of life. But the individual torn up from the roots cannot live without them. In this way, the number of those who can even understand what is at stake is being reduced.

In the work mentioned previously, A. Görres says: "If theology . . . but, above all, if the young theologian can no longer affirm the meaning and relative appropriateness of celibacy, then the *psychological* conditions that are *indispensable* for its mastery and fruitfulness are lost."[20] A very serious statement. The celibate priesthood is a noble fruit of long cultivation that withers in blighted soil. The possibility is already conceivable that, under this sad pressure, the fulfillment of it would no longer be obligatory, and this would lead to a tremendous loss of substance in the Church. We are well aware of the shortcomings of our clergy—but in tension with their high ideal [of the priesthood]. Perhaps the people of the Church will soon have to resign themselves *in principle* to a flattened, flaccid, bland type of priest until the spiral of history takes its next turn. Such a descent *cannot* be compared with the figures of married priests in the Eastern church or the Protestant vicarage, formed over long periods of time. But for all that, do not be deceived: it would bring about even worse declines, reinforcing the barbarization of eros and, among the laity, marital

[20] Albert Görres, "Psychologische", 132, emphasis added by Ida Görres.

decay—although the model of new "ideal marriages" (*Ideal-Ehen*) would be proclaimed.[21]

Our future rests on the few who fit the profound words of Bishop Hélder Câmara: "Today, as yesterday and always, mankind is led by *Abrahamic minorities* who dare to hope against all hope."[22]

III

If one has to say something in just a few lines on this complicated and multifaceted subject, it is this: in today's general discussion about priests, we repeatedly notice the astounding factual ignorance of many of those involved.

They talk as if the Catholic priesthood were still something fluid, vague, and untested, a project that has undoubtedly been a failure so far, waiting only for the layman to massage it with a firm grasp and, of course, much better insight, to fit his wishes. For example, the priest is broken down into "functions", the way one slices a roast, in order to distribute the pieces; in fact, sometimes the grim scene comes to mind of how greedy heirs around the bed of a dying man can hardly wait for the distribution of his valuables. People rave about weekend priests and part-time priests, about temporary priests, priests who have a sensible

[21] With her term "ideal marriages", Görres is expressing that what many people understood by the term "marriage" was an abstract ideal and something quite different from the Catholic teaching about what marriage is. She was acutely aware that her society's ideas about what marriage is were splintering in multiple directions at once. As she observes in her book from 1971, *What Binds Marriage Forever*, "The word 'marriage,' which was still a clear concept yesterday, wavers and fluctuates elusively today."

[22] Görres paraphrases Câmara, who writes, "I see . . . prophetic minorities, which I call Abrahamic because, like Abraham, they hope against all hope." *Helder Camara*, LADOC "Keyhole" Series 12 (Washington, D.C.: Latin America Documentation, 1975), 44.

middle-class primary job, of course with a family, and who still do a few ritual duties on the side in the evenings and on Sundays. Such wishful thinking seems to be closely related to another model of purely functional thinking and probably comes from the same root: that the mother, for example, is an old-fashioned, outdated figure, dispensable and replaceable except for the act of birth, after which she should humbly step down. All their other functions—nurturing, caring, tending, early education, and so forth—have long been performed by individuals, yet as "skills", and are therefore much better taken care of by specialists. Thus, nurses, kindergarten teachers, cooks, and so on, should preferably be described as "mothers" and should no longer put up with the fact that the woman who merely gives birth is put on a sentimental pedestal and surrounded with honor and dignity.

The priest, too, is different and more than just the accumulation of his individual functions. Of course, sacred service also consists of "natural" activities, such as speaking, praying, teaching, listening, counseling, and so forth, which laypeople can also "perform" *individually*, and, under certain circumstances, even better—though this is no reason to slaughter and dismember.

The priest is a figure and a presence—namely, one who bears an image that radiates through him and a placeholder for the figure and presence of the Lord in His Church. And this in a very definite *different* way from the way "being a representative" is incumbent on every Christian through membership and discipleship—namely, through his *ministerial office*, that is, his perpetual commission to carry out certain modes of effecting grace visibly under the authority of Christ. This authority and power to carry it out flow unceasingly "from above",[23] from Christ through the riverbed passageway of the Apostles and their successors, branching out indefinitely for twenty centuries until it reaches us; it is not generated and distributed "from below", from the community itself. "Christ is . . . the grace of God made flesh, made visible, made historical, made spatio-temporally tangible."[24] ["]The Church is the realm of His tangible presence in Word and sacrament. The priest is the person called by Him, appointed by the Church with authority, through whom this reality of God will . . .["][25] "remain present in every place and at every time until Christ comes again."[26] One can read about this (in much more detail!) in Karl Rahner, "The Parish Priest", in *Mission and Grace*—everyone who speaks up about this is strongly encouraged to read this. The conversation could gain a lot in reason and objectivity and lose some of the feeling of being in fog. "The priest is . . . sacrificer and pastor, cult-man *and* apostle, mystic . . . steward and dispenser of the mysteries of God."[27]

[23] Jas 1:17.

[24] Karl Rahner, "The Parish Priest", in *Mission and Grace: Essays in Pastoral Theology*, trans. Cecily Hastings and Richard Strachan (London: Sheed and Ward, 1963), 2:38.

[25] Görres includes the whole passage from "Christ is . . . the grace of God" to "dispenser of the mystery of God" in one set of quotation marks, as if this whole passage were from Rahner's essay "The Parish Priest". I was unable, however, to find these middle two sentences, from "The Church" to "God will," in either the original German text or in the English translation by Hastings and Strachan.

[26] Rahner, "The Parish Priest", 2:43.

[27] Rahner, "The Parish Priest", 2:43, emphasis added by Görres. The word that Hastings and Strachan translate as "cult-man" in "The Parish Priest" means the officiant at a ritual, the officiant of a cult—that is, the one who carries out the liturgy (*Liturge*).

This includes the unceasing concern that those mysteries also "arrive", that they can be prepared, grasped, deepened, taken in, embodied. In our world, there is an immense extent to which almost nothing reinforces, illustrates, supplements the Message of God and conduct that corresponds to it; rather, almost everything challenges and denies it. This part of pastoral care, the "translation" of faith into language of the era, can be quite an "exhausting" task. As a result, the homily at Mass, for example, becomes a more urgent priestly duty than ever. The whole world roars with the turmoil of youth whose fathers, in childhood and now, did not and do not have enough time for them; millions of marriages are breaking up all around because the husband, devoured by his job, neglects his wife. And in this situation, some seriously suggest that people who, with the greatest of effort (and often in vain!), can apparently deal sufficiently with only a narrow circle of three to ten people should spend weekends, as recreational amateurs, addressing the interior and exterior needs of a community of thousands of strangers on a weekly basis!

Admittedly, these questionable proposals neither fell from Heaven nor came steaming up out of Hell. And they were not hatched only by armchair theologians, in honest, if somewhat short-lived, zeal for pastoral care. A powerful reason for such hypothetical proposals is undoubtedly the massive lesson before people's eyes from grim experience that calls for a remedy. Anger about it makes the step from emotion to theory quickly enough in intelligent brains. There was and still is the *lazy* priest—a nuisance, unfortunately, as serious as the unchaste one, who makes celibacy suspect. He stands next to our priests, who are collapsing from overload, as if he lived in another world. He really just "discharges" his "few liturgical functions", and these he does sloppily, unlovingly, and to save as much time as possible. He fills the empty time in between with leisurely idleness—partly with those hobbies that, for others, are necessary relaxation but that take up an impermissible amount of room here—be they photography or music, sports, travel, television, or visits to people, which are often cultivated under the guise of spiritual zeal but which serve mainly as social entertainment. Others of this kind keep themselves busy in the way people are always on the move, with superfluous meetings, conferences, lectures, articles, with hyped-up and artificially exaggerated problems that have to be scattered as fatal seeds far and wide. It is such types that, on the one hand, make the frequently mentioned shortage of priests lack credibility and, on the other hand, almost suggest the idea of "divvying up functions". Sadly, one can understand that young theologians, in the face of such phenomena, impetuously demand to "learn something more worthwhile" on the side because they simply cannot imagine how such a meager routine could fully demand their energies primed for battle and action. And many a layman thinks that he could manage a little bit of cultic business with religious idle time in it just as well, with his left hand, and maybe even do it better.

The responsibility of Church superiors in the allocation of tasks is difficult here.

The realization of how much priestly existence decays, yes, in the double sense of the phrase "goes bad", takes center stage when a priest—whether voluntarily or also by the wrong assignment from superiors!—is restricted to only *one* of his official tasks, to the complete atrophy of the others. Perhaps no profession tolerates so badly pure specialization, which means here a splitting apart that mutilates it. The call for the half-time and quarter-time priest, or the "temporary priest", probably comes from the ranks of those who are half-employed or who are engaged in nonpriestly work, who are overwhelmed in a lopsided way, as well as from the (probably not very large) front of those laypeople whose childlike "me too, me too!" does not tolerate differentiation of status even in religious affairs—and, even there, thinks of them only as signs of prestige, equality, and success.

We are *not* talking here about the deacon, who is precisely *no* longer a layman, but participates in the priestly office in the third degree. In today's "calls for deacons" there are also—note: *also!*—certain dubious, insincere overtones and undertones that seek to turn this movement into a pretext and an instrument of a far-reaching, exceedingly adept, antipriest strategy. But here, too, no abuse changes the actual meaning and core of the calling, with which the Church is ready to try again.

Second, we are not talking *here* about the possibility, which is very worthy of consideration, that in a *real* emergency—which can even affect entire regions—in the event of a shortage of priests that cannot be remedied in any other way, worthy and suitable fathers of families could also be ordained priests. There is a huge difference between such men wanting generously to sacrifice their limited free time to the service of the Church in addition to their jobs and families versus demanding the "priest as a civilian profession" *so that he finally "also* has something real to do" and can legitimize himself only in this way as a fully useful member of society.

It is a completely *different* question—an important and worthy one, however—what kind of ecclesiastical tasks can be taken over by laymen as a substitute, in the event of *a shortage of priests that cannot be remedied in any other way* (for example, by a more reasonable use of the available ones, something still dealt with very inadequately in our country): as a state of emergency, not as a norm, as a workaround, not as a prestigious goal. We do not live in South America; we do not need it as our model. Never before has our awareness of the independent, irreplaceable tasks of the *laity* in and for the world been sharpened so much: Do we really have to strive to force ourselves into the narrowest of duties belonging to the priest—for example, preaching from the pulpit? Why should we put our own burning tasks into second place behind presumptuous ones that belong to someone else?

Since the dawn of cultures, people have appointed for every basic need of the community, for every necessary and honorable area of life, those who had to administer and represent [the community] full-time and in a way that was universally recognizable—health, law, science, education, defense, and so on.

Anyone for whom the affairs of the Kingdom of God do not seem as important as even those of doctors, judges, and teachers, who is convinced that they could be dealt with in an ancillary way and on the side, without people whose whole lives are entrusted to this task, should explore just how substantial the cause of God is for him and everyone else. For this reason alone, more so than for each of his individual functions, the priest is irreplaceable as a constant likeness and presence of God's message to us. Providing such representation, however, demands an existence filled entirely by this role, an irrevocable, uniquely suited existence.

6

Trusting the Church

Talking publicly about this topic requires overcoming more inhibitions than just stage fright. This stems from respect for the topic and respect for the listeners, from a concern about not doing them both justice.

The topic this evening is a particular challenge: not because of the audience but because of this era and each person's own heart and mind. After all, who dares to ask the question: "Do you trust the Church? Do you yourself trust the Church?" And not with short-term caution—for example: "Do you still trust? Still today?"—but entirely and in general, yesterday, today, and until death. Who dares to ask this if not a person who has affirmed the question himself with a pure yes? But how difficult it is to justify such a yes.

The fact that I come before you with this does not serve, of course, as a personal outpouring in the style of well-known pious groups from Oxford or Geneva. How did I get here, and, especially, how did you get here? I can refer to Newman, who is said to have commented, "Sharing mere private views, which I think no one else holds but me, makes me feel like a juggler who entertains people with his leaps at the market."[1] Rather, I think that with what follows I speak on behalf of many who remain silent or are at a loss for words, but not as a criticism of their attitude, least of all in

[1] I have not been able to find such a reference in the works of Newman.

our overly loud, verbose time. Many years ago, a theologian said to me, "Faith makes mute, unbelief makes eloquent", which is certainly often, if not always, true, the way love also makes some mute, while seduction usually requires a well-trained eloquence. And it is precisely in our current ecclesiastical confusion that many serious, deeply engaged people know how to reply in the face of the overwhelming theological opinion only with concerned silence. This in no way indicates that they have no ideas or that they lack responses. Newman has a whole book showing how much genuine faith there is that *has* reasons but is not reflected in and certainly not empowered through words.[2]

It is on behalf of such people that I would now like to speak to you.

Much of the criticism is certainly incomplete and, even when justified, for many it is unsatisfying. During the whole painstaking reflection on this ahead of time, I kept seeing the image of a huge ball of mercury, slipping away from any grasp—because it is a single whole that we have to talk about, and it is one; it is one thing with immense variety and complexity, and a whole that cannot be sliced up and presented piece by piece (at least not by me). Each selection is arbitrary and lacks important information; every fragment is understandable only against a well-thought-out background.

So, trusting the Church: today, in the turmoil, in the confusion, in the dissolving of clear boundaries, in the shouting of demands and claims, in the wavering of principles, in the extinguishing of ancient lights, in the breaking down of walls, in the drying up of the old wells. Trusting the Church

[2] Görres is probably referring to John Henry Newman, *An Essay in Aid of a Grammar of Assent* (1870).

as if this crisis might be a fever but a healing deliverance at the same time.

Does not every act of trusting, consciously or unconsciously, presuppose something solid, something strong and powerful? Something that assuredly, protectively, and reliably enables us to partake?

But what is still firm and tranquil today in the Church, in Christianity, in our faith? What does not waver and wobble? What is not being challenged from the outside and, most harshly, from the inside by theologians, by priests?

Does this not apply even to the most basic principles? Let us pick just a few:

The Ten Commandments: a grim anecdote comes to mind that Ortega y Gasset told fifty years ago, of the gypsy who, when asked about her knowledge, dodges the question: "I wanted to learn [the Commandments]; I heard rumormongering, I heard they would be done away with; I let them be!"[3] That is how far we have come. It is said that the new catechism presents only ten words to schoolchildren—impeccably philological, is it not, according to the Decalogue—but by no means compulsory: nice ideal concepts, ethical dreamy aspirations, but that is not how reality is.

The Creed: each and every part is contested. It is treated as cumbersome. It is cleverly and eruditely negated; it is deleted or "reinterpreted". God the Creator and Incarnation,

[3] The context of this anecdote: "The gypsy in the story went to confession, but the cautious priest asked him if he knew the Commandments of the Law of God. To which the gypsy replied, 'Well, Father, it's this way: I *was* going to learn them, but I heard talk that they were going to do away with them.' Is not this the situation in the world at present? The rumour is running round that the commandments of the law of Europe are no longer in force, and in view of this, men and peoples are taking the opportunity of living without imperatives." José Ortega y Gasset, *The Revolt of the Masses* (New York: W. W. Norton, 1932), 135.

the God-Man, born of the Virgin Mary; our salvation through His Cross, Resurrection, and Ascension; the Second Coming; the holy catholic and apostolic Church, her birth from the Spirit, her completion at the end of time; eternal life in Heaven and Hell; and the New Earth.

Everything is denied, rejected, ridiculed—not by officially godless people, but by consecrated priests, by theologians, preachers, pastors appointed to preach.

The sacraments? Misunderstanding and magic are most of what we believed: of baptism, especially baptism of children through water and Word and Spirit; of the Real Presence, the Consecration of the Eucharist; of ordination, which priests themselves passionately deny, rejecting the rite as a farce; what are confirmation and anointing of the sick when the laying on of hands and anointing are also just magical remnants from various forms of paganism? Confession: for the first time in some dioceses this year, children were led to First Communion without this; when a child asked, "And what do I do with my sins?" the pastor replied, "I don't care about your sins"; this is exactly the same answer that a relative of mine received when, getting married late in life, he wanted to make a general confession before the wedding. As if, until now, we had confessed in order to share some interesting gossip for the curiosity of the priests! Marriage is to be "reformed" so that it can be revoked, with the possibility of repetition, and in marriage, practices are to be permitted that every form of paganism, pre- and post-Christian, has cooked up but are an abomination to the Hindus and pious Jews. The state of holy orders loses its foundation and its roots when the concept of the evangelical counsels is lost, along with the sense of sacrifice and virginity. Monks run away on all sides, abbots marry—and, more incomprehensible than these events: the highest authority in Rome also legalizes such conditions.

Angels and devils have been abolished with laughter; veneration of saints is so taboo that one has to bring the pious Reformed pastor Walter Nigg from Zurich to Germany if an anniversary calls for a lecture, as if no priest among us had the knowledge or courage for such a topic.

With the belief in the Eucharist, of course, building tents for the Presence of Christ among us, "houses of God", loses any meaning that would go beyond the parish hall, which is consequently required to be a "multipurpose building" for political discussion and with all the comforts for chatting, smoking, and even dancing, as a student chaplain recently explicitly and literally called for. Logically, of course, the cemeteries, the fields of God, too—what embarrassingly magical words!—must be liquidated and the corpses handed over to the trash removal without any big to-do. In this regard, there is still some inconsistency.

It is not only small groups of intellectuals who are hacking at the roots as well as the branches of the tree of faith. They have gotten down into the smallest "Catholic" publications, church bulletins and women's group newsletters, eager to be henchmen who, with their combined strength, distance themselves from the old-fashioned, idiotic stupidity of previous beliefs.

Whom should we trust? A theology that continually explains its own bankruptcy via leading speakers; an interpretation of revelation that turns it into a rather unimportant science, destroying its own foundations, rejects Tradition, dissolves the Bible, denies the highest Magisterium, and, finally, as the capstone of their wisdom, invents absolute blasphemy, unutterable by any Jew, Muslim, or Gentile, which one can quote only to report on and say with physical reluctance: "God is dead"? (But their unfortunately endless production fills the shelves of Christian bookstores very profitably.)

Which theologian can one read carefully and without reservations, without being so on edge that it hurts, holding one's breath tensely? And when you are happy and grateful—do you know what he will say tomorrow?

Every twist, every excess seems conceivable, seems possible—for the noblest as well as the basest motives. Yes, even for the noblest, because the burning zeal to understand even the erring brother compels some to go not only two miles instead of just one but up to and over the limit; because some who want to throw off Tradition and faith are willing not only to offer their coat as well as their cloak but also to tear off their skin as a sign of fraternal solidarity to satisfy them.[4] Only God can judge what is happening here. Personally, this may be enough for some to be holy. But the calamity of the frustration for the little people, the confusion into which they plunge, is at the same time enormous.

Whom should we trust? A morality that willingly and complacently adapts to all the developments of everyday behavior, justifying everything, if possible, that fears nothing as much as a distinct separation of good and evil, as much as a clear *non licet* [not allowed], conforming anxiously to the zeitgeist, attentive to the approval of the greatest number?

Whom should we trust?

A liturgical reform that comes from the highest legitimate authorities of the Church, undoubtedly from the best intention of the supporters, who have indeed given us some beautiful, precious, fruitful innovations—nevertheless frighten-

[4] See Mt 5:40–41.

ingly shot through by tendencies clearly of foreign origin, too willing to make compromises and concessions to certain cliques and their followers that, in hard-to-comprehend accommodations to overt as well as subtle demands, gradually cut through many fine, unnoticed roots that anchored general worship in the hearts of the people and nourished Catholic piety: fasting and feast days, customs and traditions, oral prayers and gestures of prayer, the mourning of Good Friday, the expression of the compassion of the Church with the human pain of separation in the use of black for the liturgy of the dead (not the annual commemorations!), the sustained familiar recurrence of the annual readings, the rhythm of which was still one of the few living harmonies with the Protestant church, like the Kyrie with the Eastern one?(And this is in the ecumenical age!) Lots of small, petty interventions, strange unimportant ones, that dismantle an irreplaceable, gradually matured habit of prayer and literally spoil the worship service for countless believers?

Whom should we trust?

"Ministers" who vehemently no longer want to be priests, who deny the name itself as a pagan relic, who want to be merely functionaries, nothing different from the layperson, functionaries with a right to resign, on a part-time basis, as a side job? Clerics, whose self-diminishment and desertion disgusts even outsiders, clerics who constantly explain to us out loud what their service is *not* worth to them, the importance of which they measure against subjective "happiness" claims, who fear nothing so much as to be recognized as a Catholic priest, assiduously hiding this affiliation, and who no longer want to acknowledge their status as such; clerics whom one would be embarrassed to ask for their blessing?

We are so used to everything, so hardened, that nothing surprises us anymore. If we do not hear for a while from friends who are a married couple, we do not usually worry and ask ourselves: "Do they still live together? Are they already divorced and remarried?" But I have to confess: if I do not hear from a chaplain friend for half a year, I get worried: "Is he still with us? Did he get married in the end?"

The elderly painfully remember the years of the Third Reich, the war—the situation of constant rumors, the shocking revelations: "Have you heard?" At that time, there was talk of the fallen and the arrested; today, of those who have fallen away, been seduced, done a U-turn; then, bombs and devastation; today, scandal and abominations in the sanctuary. Yes, really, abominations—and today as it was then: if one rejected something too extreme, too drastic, as if it must be just a tendentious tale, it turned out to be true afterward: the story of the religion teacher who told children to bring their rosaries, little images of saints, and religious medals to school, and then commanded them to burn all of them; the report from the Dutch pastor who married two homosexual men in church; from the Sunday sermon in which the words "Jesus Christ was not the Son of God, but a poor devil like us; this is the truth" were said.

In the Third Reich, external persecution united believers firmly and faithfully. The new confusion divides families, monasteries, homes, old circles of friends. People are isolated and feel abandoned in their parishes, more so than they ever did before in the unbelieving environment of their workplaces. Many letters, many conversations bear witness to this.

Whom should we trust?

Even where we find unshaken loyalty to the whole faith of the Church and her pastors: Is not the milieu, the situation, there often even more problematic?

Our Confiteor cannot be honest and thorough enough.

Do you not understand from the bottom of your soul that a lot of young people who are honest seekers would not even think of looking for the living reality of God here? Do people not understand that the thousandfold impulses to disappointment, indignation, flight, or resignation are, in fact, a reaction to the many spectacles: everything that the world in its schadenfreude has always criticized about the pious—dreariness and stubbornness, boundless blindness to the pressing needs, resentment, stagnation, severity, and dishonesty? How few are really affected by the movement of the Spirit, how much shadow play, sloganeering, and patching together fake exteriors there is!

Do we have even one monastery with the radiance of Taizé? Do we have even one publication of clear, distinctive character, of *niveau*, fire, and heft, that meets the unbelievable cheek of penetrating unbelief with calm, fearless, engaging superiority?

Whom can we trust?

Our bishops are, thank God, without exception, honorable, irreproachable men. But do you have the impression that they are up to the situation, even superior to it? Even with the best will, the answer is no—you can feel a painful, pitiful helplessness and feel that they are at a loss. Of course, we cannot demand strategic ingenuity as proof of proficiency in the pastoral office—but how longingly we look for at least one who passes from hesitant defense to enlightened, enlightening initiative! If power means being *able* to protect, preserve, prevent—enforce commandments and prohibitions—then the ecclesiastical authorities were far from being so powerless. The behavior of the rebellious clergy, even those who disobey calmly, shows this most clearly. No school class behaves like this with a teacher who actually has authority, who does not just deputize it.

And our Holy Father—I purposely choose this lofty name, which expresses the longing of all mankind, especially in an era of fatherlessness—he, too, is an honorable and venerable person, but he is truly overloaded beyond the limits of what is humanly possible.[5] He simply *cannot* conduct himself properly continuously and everywhere—no one could; he, too, is bound to swerve and get sidetracked. And every sign of his weakness is immediately trumpeted around the world with tremendous glee. (I do not mean, by the way, the encyclical *Humanae vitae*, which I, on the contrary, consider to be a great prophetic act—only posterity will do it justice—but here, too, the message was mingled with such hapless phrases that it opened itself to cheap criticism, factually honest as well as infamous.) Even with him, we always have to fear and hope and pray that he will not make disastrous mistakes that do more harm than good.

Where is there a prophet in Israel?[6]

If we consider the almost absolute trust that the fully committed, reverent, grateful, and obedient people of faith have been accustomed to give to the Church, and especially to her priests, only then can we measure the disaster that shock, poisoning, and ostracism in the depths of the soul has brought to these people.

This attitude was by no means just a form of stupidity, a result of stuck-in-the-mud naivety, infantility, servility in the face of feudalistic-paternalistic authority, threats of the hereafter, and the way that whole ignorant, belittling gibberish goes. Certainly, such did exist, as a matter of course and inevitable incidental factors. But those who despised these

[5] Pope Paul VI.

[6] See 2 Kings 3:11.

people completely failed to discern the heart of the matter. It was something vast and unique. It was the last manifestation in that realm we know of the great ancient trust in the world, the harmony of the individual with his comprehensive divinely ordained order, the grace-enabled transposition of pagan trust in the cosmos into the New Creation. The attempt in the name of enlightenment, ameliorating Catholic backwardness, maturity of the laity, and so on not to shine light on this unspeakably deep, happiness-generating, mysterious anchor but, rather, to smash it with an ax and a hammer is an assassination attempt on a most precious legacy of the world. It is a form of outright soul murder, and not only to individuals—it is a spiritual genocide.

Is it any wonder when the worst, creeping fear sometimes invades even people of the best intention, in quiet hours, in the silence of sleepless nights: What if they might be right? There are so many, such smart people among them, in such high, responsible positions, priests and laypeople! Can I alone be right against this throng of opposing witnesses? Against this immense flood, which is bursting forth out of the mass media—not least of all in Church radio and in printed works with ecclesial imprimaturs and financed by the hierarchy? What am I, a poor individual, to do against a power that even the bishops seem to tremble at and tiptoe around?

What if the rebels really were to own the future? What if this process, which seems to us like destruction and betrayal, were actually God's Will and to resist it were impious and an act of petty faith? What if—an agonizing thought in the midnight hours—what if I were tied to a great but inexorably dying body, through merely emotionally stirring but ultimately subjective, unreasonable inhibitions, habits, prejudices, antiquated piety, wrongly grounded loyalty? What if the people from whom we received faith and guidance were themselves blind guides for the blind?

Are we living on a leaky ship sinking inch by inch, from which not only the rats but also the sensible, sober people jump off just in time?

Who provides an answer for us in such hours? Whom else can we ask?

Only the Church herself.

Only the great, the whole, the long-lived, immortal on earth, the one that is identical with her own beginning, that is also identical with her Lord in a manner befitting her alone—because, in spite of all the fashionable concerns about this terrifyingly weighty discourse of older theology, she is nevertheless the "continually living Christ", who speaks and responds to us in the Church as the place of His grace, as His custodian. The recipient of that rock-solid trust of our fathers *is still the same one.*

The Church: the word, of course, is used in its old full sense, which means not only the temporal segment of the Catholics living today. It is not a system, an idea, an ideology, a structure, a society, rather the tremendous living establishment, which has existed since the Apostles until today, fulfilling her history from century to century, growing, unfolding, struggling, ailing, recovering, living out her destiny and maturing toward the return of the Lord.

[She is] the strangest creation of God, so unique in kind, so large, so contradictory, so colorful that no single person can take stock of her and figure her out, and certainly no outsider can ever take her all in, let alone understand her and judge her. Only she herself can do this, comprehending herself in faith, endlessly considering herself in her faithful theology, looking at herself through her mystics, loving herself in her children. Only the believer *as* the cell of this body, embedded, suffused with her life-process of knowledge, faith, love, participates also in her consciousness and in the spirit in which she understands herself.

Her secret and what can be offensive about her (as with her Lord: "And blessed is he who takes no offense at me"![7]) reside in her *twofold nature*. In terms of her empirical visibility, concreteness, and conceivability, she, like any worldly phenomenon, is subject to the observation and analysis of history, sociology, religious studies, philosophy, and psychology, and their findings are correct in many ways. At the *same time*, she is what faith and its theology know and proclaim about her from the beginning: the People of God, the Body of Christ, the vine, the city of God, yes, the Bride; each of the visual names, symbols of inexhaustible depth of interpretation, tries in alternating cycles to stammer out the unspeakable aspect of her "second nature".

Unacceptable to the critical intellect—for certain. The critical intellect reaffirms that every day. As for Christians, however, if they take their faith seriously, it is not unlikely that they have to accept something analogous, albeit in a lesser version, *about themselves* every day.

That I am the person I am—the empirical individual, object of all the natural sciences, object also of psychology and psychoanalysis, suffering object of history and civilization, social structures, a product of ancestry, milieu, and education, on top of all the influences of the present, the decadence, the flow of suggestions in a hundred forms, conscious of my personal destiny and character, its advantages and disadvantages, its limitations, hindrances, and my failures in the middle of this: the sum of all these statements

[7] Lk 7:23.

has so much that is uplifting and valuable, so much that is shameful, unappetizing, depressing. What a concoction!

So *that* is I; that is you; that is each of us in unpredictable variations. And at the *same time*, I am supposed to believe—and I do believe: I am created in the image and likeness of God, known, wanted, loved from eternity, formed by His hands, a continuation in the whole endless stream of my heritage, every hair of my head counted. I am a brother or sister of Christ, redeemed by His blood, coheir, and aspirant to glory. I am on the way to eternal bliss—yes, the new taboos are also good for something; rarely heard words unfold their almost unbearable force again: oriented to eternal bliss in the perfect unity of God, in the physical resurrection in a New Heaven and a New Earth.

And I am supposed to believe that about myself—and everything that is seething around me? This is, however, a lot to swallow for those who are attentive and who view themselves and their loved ones even a little critically.

For those who accept this message, the double nature of the Church can be quite clear—even in today's situation.

What is more self-evident than that there is *always* an abyss gaping between the first and second basic condition of the Church? There has to be a gap, because the distance between mission and realization is too great, between the One who reveals Himself and the manifestation that proclaims Him.

Always, in every era, the earthly Church at the same time contradicts her "other", actual nature. She is always in need of reform. Her best children, the saints, are always unhappy with her and cry out in love and suffering for repentance and penance.

For me, Church history *is* the great book of consolation. It really is not just a lavish *Chronique scandaleuse* (chronicle of scandal) for ravenous agitators. Today, more than ever, it is necessary for us to be able to see through the torrent of events and even put them halfway in perspective and weigh them. The outright ignorance of an unbelievable number of otherwise educated Christians in this area counts as one of the calamities.

The darkest chapters are exactly the ones we should know—not just the boring Renaissance vices. No, we should know the great heresy battles of the early Church, the Viking and Saracen assaults at the beginning of the Middle Ages, which almost choked Christendom, barely awakened, in blood and ashes. We should know the age of the Reformation, the Enlightenment, the era of secularization, which, at the time of our great-grandparents, simply swept away a large portion of the German centers of ministry and educational institutions. We also have to unlearn confusing the "calm" times of the Church with good, and the agitated with bad.

It was Innocent III, of all people, the man who distributed the crowns of Europe from the vertiginous summit of the papacy, who saw the Church sway and crumble in a dream until a dark little stranger supported it with his shoulder—whom he then recognized in Francis. At the time of Romanticism, which was also an era of secularization but today is misunderstood by many as a Catholic heyday, Anne Catherine Emmerich saw the body of the Lord hanging on a pole—blackened, mangled, mutilated. She saw crowds, among them priests and bishops, who zealously carried away the Church of Saint Peter, stone by stone, and built an "Anti-Church" with the help of demons.[8]

Times of ascent and decay perpetually alternate—early

[8] See, for example, K. E. Schmöger, *The Life of Anne Catherine Emmerich*, vol. 1 (Rockford, Ill.: TAN Books, 1976), 475.

spring, naked, bleak, but bursting with buds, alternates with sterile, visually stunning autumn splendor. Time and again ripeness changes into apparent death, and this breaks open into new life. The Church *is* the Phoenix.

Today, it seems to me, two opposite, but often eerily similar, currents are tangled up: *renewal* and *revolution*. The two-sided nature of this, this tremendous ambiguity, is the peculiarity and the particular danger of our hour.

The key term for renewal is "the Council". This is incorrect, by the way, or let us say shallow and superficial, if one sets it as the absolute beginning. In fact, it was itself the fruit and result of a rebirth movement that was strong yet scattered widely among many small points of tension that grew out of invisible factors ("all beginnings are invisible", says Teilhard de Chardin) since about the First World War. Over a half century, brooks grew and flowed together into this basin. The Council raised, confirmed, legitimized, and radiated ideas, impulses, premonitions, and approaches, as well as ready-made formations, developed over many generations, to the awareness of the whole Church.

Just at this moment, after that long, arduous, patient preparation, the second stage of the great, indeed Spirit-led, rebirth—this is how the small charismatic circles always understood them!—that is, the second phase of general realization should, properly speaking must, follow. That was the tremendous, intoxicating hope of the [19]60s, crystallized around the shining figure of John XXIII.

And exactly here is where the counterplay, the Adversary, intrudes.

Mother Teresa of Calcutta, the great charismatic missionary, said to me a few years ago: "That the devil would try so hard to distort the meaning of the Council, to turn it upside down, suggests that it must have been a big deal."

It is becoming clearer and clearer that there is now a movement alongside, within the renewal, a movement that is not concerned with purification, strengthening, development, rebirth but, rather, with the downfall of the Church, with her replacement by an alien new structure. This truly genuine revolution uses all means of political upheaval—that is, so far with the subtler means, since it is not yet openly in power. They work with "psychic artillery": with suggestion, surprise, infiltration, and as a fifth column with an extensive strategy, occupying key positions in mass media and using sophisticated camouflage. Friedrich Heer, who ought to know, calls the method they use "Nicodemic" (why actually? poor faithful Nicodemus!).[9] That is to say, they use the vocabulary of conventional theory while, line by line, attributing alien meanings.

It seems to me that the characteristic of this revolution is that *unbelievers and the ignorant* lead the "reform" of the Church—and with great success.

Well now, this is quite strange.

The mark of previous waves of renewal in the Church was surely that they originated from piety, from repentance—that is, from an inner change oriented toward God. Sometimes they were started by saints; sometimes by Christians of more humble calling but who aligned with the spirit and model of the saints. Even with all their shortcomings and failures, the baseline of such movements nevertheless showed that, in those people, the Church herself converted in repentance from corruption, sliding off course, or slumber. There was no talk first of rights and claims, of relief and more comfortable ways, rather of willingness to bow to the gospel and its demands, of joyful submission even

[9] Regarding the "Nicodemic" method, see chapter 2, note 3.

to the strictness of the Commandments of God, of bitter purification in love and humility, in renunciation and obedience to be able to live up to the mission and rediscover the neglected legacy.

I cannot discern these features in the guise of today's revolt. Of course, there have always been unbelievers in the Church—probably in large numbers, one suspects also among priests. We know this well from some periods—for example, the High Enlightenment—from others it can be conjectured. As is well known, there is conscious theoretical and repressed but practical unbelief. I use the word "unbelieving" here with no moral judgment. In thousands of very different fates hide the innocent, the guilty, and every shade in between. I simply mean those who, for whatever reason, deny belief in or obedience to the Church, or both, and who place themselves internally or externally (or again, both) outside her—whether they were still in the parish registers as lukewarm Catholics or, in the jargon of the pious, as "non-practicing" Catholics, whether they called themselves freethinkers, free spirits, or liberals (and there were certainly priests among them). Still, the last thing they wanted was to attract attention.

They had *one* distinguishing feature in common, in spite of all their differences, and it characterized them: total disinterest in the whole of the Church's internal affairs and inner life, in dogmas and liturgy (if they knew there was such a thing), in piety as well as in religious organizations. Volunteering for such things seemed simply unspeakably boring, bourgeois, tasteless, narrow-minded; any attraction to such topics seemed to them tactless and impossible.

They did not want to have anything to do with all this, and they stuck by that. And that was fortunate, because it did not occur to them even in their sleep to interfere in Church matters and tell us how we should run them.

But this is exactly what they are doing today and with vigor. It is a strange spectacle: a number (an army or just a leadership corps?) of people who really believe only in the alternative religion of the zeitgeist—that is, in progress, science, moral autonomy, and a future paradise resulting from all three—rush upon the Church to remodel everything they find in her according to their dimensions, goals, and desires. And they want to dictate to and rule over all the other believers.

In Christianity, they find some very useful material for their undertaking, next to a huge pile of ballast—as they assess it. With unbridled energy and great intelligence, they begin to carve up some things, to recast other things, and to dissolve the rest. And they recognized in the major reform that is being set into motion—properly so, because they are least of all dumb—a splendid vehicle, and they know how to use it. To do this, they provide themselves with the necessary, thorough information in all areas—a completely new, uncanny kind of religious and theological interest.

They have many types and layers of fellow travelers and tools—on occasion, the *ignorant*; they, too, have always been in abundance in the Church. This includes both the faithful, who believed in the whole and were content with it—not in a bad way, by the way—and others who were indifferent to everything because they knew nothing, and vice versa. Both types behaved passively, leaving thinking and doing to those who were better equipped or simply appointed. Among us today, this layer still has a special historical imprint.

Remember the last thirty years: National Socialism with its monopoly on schools, media, culture, especially youth;

evacuation and cities reduced to rubble, shipping children to the countryside, compulsory participation in the Hitler Youth, mandatory labor, antiaircraft auxiliary, and so on; the complete standstill of almost all forms of advanced religious education, religious instruction reduced to a minimum, the constant change of school and teacher, and nonstop manipulation by propaganda. Afterward came debris, refugee misery, the struggle for existence of their parents' generation. The likes of this do not leave younger generations without a trace. As for those who were not among the innermost circles of pious believers at the time, who did not come to the Church later through personal conversion, somehow the newly consolidated conditions also brought masses flowing back, carried along by the current, into the Church structure, without catching up on lost foundations, without personal conviction. As previously in politics—it is clear that these people are the ones most vulnerable to the mass media. A great many remained dyed in the wool from the ideological imprint of their childhood and youth, including in what they had repressed—at least with a tremendous inclination for distrust, suspicion, criticism, and dissatisfaction with the Church and religion.

By their nature, one could say the majority of this type would probably be among the uninterested who prefer to deal with anything other than religion and what is related to it. But today, under the all-encompassing honorary title "laity", an active participation is imposed on them—on people from both currents!—something they would never have sought out. They are forcefully—from *both* sides!—talked into believing that they understand everything, even better than the experts, that they have a say in evaluating and judging even the most difficult and complicated matters. Their most random impressions and reactions are researched as extremely interesting and important and are supposed to provide norms and corrections for the established situation. It is actually grotesque. Is it not clear that they provide the real revolutionaries with just what they need—namely, gullible supporters?

There are other factors. Every revolution has to base itself on the groups of those who are *dissatisfied*. They are, of course, abundant in the Church, including among the clergy. I have already touched on the reasons. They can be multiplied endlessly, the good and the bad, from misunderstanding and from clear insight, out of actual negative experiences and in the spirit of going along with the crowd.

There is the urgent unrest of those who are truly religiously moved and religiously gifted. There is the dull, irritated resentment of those who believe that Church authorities prevent them from fulfilling their personal happiness—for example, in marriage, ambition, or other private interests. Everyone will pay attention when someone promises to be responsive to their complaints, to stop what bothers them quickly, to fulfill their wishes.

Here everything is mixed in. There may be many who would have dedicated themselves to genuine renewal with enthusiasm if they had encountered it. Or they were deceived. The front lines of those who sought both to preserve and renew appeared to them—rightly or wrongly!—too lukewarm, too dawdling, too willing to compromise, too petty, too careful. How very understandable in so many situations! They throw themselves into the arms of those who promise them direct action and rapid radical overhaul, who appeal to the jam-packed explosive vigor of the youth.

This is how the corrupters reach out to many—to useful people with more passion than discretion, more anger than patience, perhaps also more desire for validation and assertiveness than willingness to accept their integration into the Church and to sacrifice themselves. There are also those who are just naive, willing to trust, easy to deceive—all of whom, in character and vocation, genuinely belonged to the Church's actual rebirth movement and are severely lacking among us.

I see the treacherous, the grueling aspect of our situation in the fact that the two fundamentally contradictory currents seem to intersect, overlap, get tangled up, even seem to merge in aggrandized speech and writing—often on the same page, even in the same person!—so much so that a clear distinction at first glance and in all areas is simply not possible. Oh, how much we need to pray for discernment of spirits, just to hang in there day after day! We certainly notice this when it comes down, plain and simple, to the basics. But they are not always directly at play. The lines of approach—for defense as well as for offense—are often lengthy and convoluted. Also, a house does not consist only of its foundation, and a person does not consist only of his skeleton. Both can still be intact while the dissolution, the disfigurement, has already progressed considerably. And how unmanageable is the potential variety in development of often inconspicuous points of departure! How imperceptible are built-in timed fuses and creeping infections!

Perhaps—probably—this terrible lack of transparency also plays a role in the often-strange attitude of our hierarchy during this "soft upsurge". (I say "also"—and plays "along"!) One never knows. Does it have to do with the Lord's words about leaving the weeds until the harvest, about leaving the dimly burning wick and the bent reed?[10] Or is it an expression of uncertainty and indecision, a tactical retreat, a fearful attempt at compromise—or even unconscious infiltration of some officially rejected ideology?

With a slight horror, one often thinks of Ernst Jünger's remark: "the measure of a metaphysical attack" is that its "irresistible force rests in the fact that the target itself, apparently willingly, chooses the means of its demise".[11]

A rather dark image. And what about that which is holy coming out of the crisis?

I believe in this. I believe with confidence and trust in the indestructible future of the old and the new, the one, holy, catholic, and apostolic Church. Now we are simply being put to the test whether we take seriously the Lord's Sermon on the Mount and [His assertion] that the gates of Hell will not prevail against [the Church].

The prognoses are, of course, very bad, according to human judgment. Seduction and decay have by no means reached their full velocity; many dragon teeth have only just been inserted. The defense is mostly as weak as the anti-aircraft guns in our cities were when faced with a huge squadron of bombers. Based on calculations, we would probably need to pack up soon.

How are things looking with our young priests, for example—in number and quality? What can we expect? How about our theology departments? As with the relevant literature—one does not want to call it "Catholic" anymore. Thank God I have nothing to do with school and teaching,

[10] See Mt 13:24–30; 12:20; Is 42:3.

[11] Ernst Jünger, *The Worker: Dominion and Form*, ed. Laurence Paul Hemming, trans. Laurence Paul Hemming and Bogdan Costea (Evanston, Ill.: Northwestern University Press, 2017), 103.

but samples and assessments—that is, praise and acclaim as well as horrified warnings—about the new catechism and its additions can prepare us for a rather dark harvest. A generation of those who are essentially skeptics, grumblers, as well as arrogant and irreverent meddlers appears to be involved.

I can very well imagine that tomorrow will be pitch-black. For example, to start with the smaller issues, I can imagine that old churches will, in fact, be transformed into mere museums and new ones will be built with bars and dance programs. Home Masses (sorry, eucharistic celebrations) with champagne breakfasts at the same table are already in vogue—exactly what Paul, greatly displeased, did away with.[12]

I can imagine that the *appearance* of the Church, deprived of all the beautiful traditions, the liturgical spaces, vestments, vessels, customs, places of pilgrimage, most of the monasteries, and other "magical remains", will resemble an ugly, hewn willow stump. The City on the Hill will be reduced to the ruins of the city wall, devoid of its shining light that once irresistibly attracted so many seekers from afar. I can also imagine that in some areas, after some time, the Catholic Church will continue only by vegetating as a shabby variation of the neighboring Protestant church. It will not even be like the solid state church or an authentic living sect but only as a slavish copy of figures gutted and in decay. I can imagine a widely denied but practically implemented schism, connected to Rome only by insincere verbal threads—and unfortunately without a clean cut from there [that is, from Rome] through the Gordian knot.

I also know that in view of these (and other) conditions, some people who are to be taken seriously consider apoc-

[12] See 1 Cor 11:27–30.

alyptic fulfillment to have come, and they prepare for the end of all things, not just of Germany or Europe or the white race. What can I say? I can understand this even if I do not share this opinion. We have long since deserved this. However, Philipp Dessauer used to say, "The last day has many dress rehearsals." And we have been told that it will surprise us.[13]

As I said: I can imagine the darkest development, and I also expect it.

Yet, I, by no means, believe, first, that it *must* happen, and second, that it will come to stay. Is world history not already full of great surprises, despite the cleverest predictions? Is it not full of sudden reversals, wonderful rescues, incomprehensible victories of small groups of fighters against unlikely odds? In no way has God always been on the side of the strongest cannons. Think of Salamis and the fall of the Persian fleet, the mysterious retreat of the Mongols in the middle of their victory at Wahlstatt, the strange fates in the struggle of the West with the Turks—at the Gates of Vienna, in Corfu—and the tiny, almost invisible origins of world-threatening powers such as the Nazis and the Bolsheviks out of ridiculed, weak groups.[14] Good and evil make the strangest leaps—even in the most profane realms of military power, politics, and economics. How can one then think accurately to predict the fate of the spiritual struggle—in which, as we know, not only flesh and blood but very different powers and forces are involved[15]—on both sides!

[13] See Matt 24:36.

[14] Battle of Salamis, 480 B.C. Battle of Wahlstatt (also known as the Battle of Legnica), 1241. Battle at the Gates of Vienna: the most significant of several such battles was in 1683. Siege of Corfu, 1576 or 1716.

[15] See Eph 6:12.

To start with the simplest aspect: as for those of us who believe we are on the right side by God's grace and the people we trust—do we all come from "ideal religious backgrounds"? Probably only a small portion. Think how many of us who have come from lukewarm to unbelieving families are converts, grew up under annoying priests, with miserable religious instruction, worse than inadequate pastoral care, dreadful sermons, neglected or even twisted liturgy, uptight religious education at home or in boarding schools attached to religious orders. And after our conversions and renewals, think what else we ran into, what kind of dead ends. Think how often we had to break out of unbearable situations, how often were we peeled down to the skin—and this on top of everything else. Did we fall from God's hand for even a moment?[16] Did He not send us His angels at the crossroad—even in strange disguises—or the raven with bread?[17] Did He not strike open a spring out of sand and stone in the desert?[18] How could He deny His Church what He does for us gnats, does every day?

I believe in God's faithfulness.

And I just do not believe that the Holy Spirit will abandon His own Pentecost-like flare-up, the great promise of the Council, to poisoning and distortion—unless it were to happen through our own outsized fault if we were to surrender prematurely.

I trust the Church's tremendous powers of regeneration—they will be awakened when the need is at its greatest. Pre-

[16] See Jn 10:28–29.

[17] As for "angels at the crossroads" who are not recognized, Görres may be alluding to Genesis 18:1–33; 19:1–3; Judges 6:11–24; 13:1–25; or Hebrews 13:2. In addition, other passages in the Bible mention angels, recognized as such, who come to help. As for the raven, see 1 Kings 17:6.

[18] See Exodus 17:6; Num 20:1–13; Ps 78:15; 105:41.

cisely because she is a poor Bride in misery now, she is more at the mercy of His grace than ever.

I trust in her invisible allies, in the communion of saints in the old sense, in which we who are living are only a tiny part, embedded in the old image of the "three-story" Church: we the struggling, pilgrim Church between the suffering, where there is purification, and the triumphant (yes, in spite of the foolish narrowing of this forbidden word!), the Church of Heaven, perfected in the victory of Christ. With them in mind, not only the solitary Christian facing the pressure of external persecution but also the one almost despondent in the internal pressure of isolation, I can answer with Thomas More, as he did when his judges, alluding to their numerical advantage, urged him to conform: "From among the holy bishops, I can oppose any of your hundred. For this one council or parliament (and God knows what kind it is!), there are all the councils over a thousand years. This is why I am not obliged to conform my conscience to the council (synod) of a single country."[19]

[19] This is a paraphrase from a passage of Saint Thomas More's speech at his trial in 1535:

> If the number of bishops and universities should be so material as your lordship seems to think, then I see little cause, my lord, why that should make any change in my conscience. For I have no doubt that, though not in this realm, but of all those well learned bishops and virtuous men that are yet alive throughout Christendom, they are not fewer who are of my mind therein. But if I should speak of those who are already dead, of whom many are now holy saints in heaven, I am very sure it is the far greater part of them who, all the while they lived, thought in this case the way that I think now. And therefore am I not bound, my lord, to conform my conscience to the council of one realm against the General Council of Christendom.

Gerard B. Wegemer, *Thomas More: A Portrait of Courage* (New York: Scepter Publishers, 1995), 216.

I believe and trust that even the ugliest and worst manifestations of this revolution represent phases of a necessary self-cleansing of the Church body and at the same time a well-deserved judgment. As Anne Catherine Emmerich said about her nightmarish visions of apostasy and betrayal in the Church, "It is good that there are such people. They drive the matter forward, and finally it erupts. And then good and evil part ways." The invaders may have a role similar to that of the Assyrians and Babylonians in obstinate Israel. And at revolutionary tribunals, alongside the innocents, real guilt is called out.

Even more, I trust the *suffering* in the Church. There is immense suffering, silent and down to the foundations—above all, the suffering among the many, many good, faithful priests, who hardly appear in the press and on television but who, with the commitment of their lives, known only to those close to them, are consumed for those entrusted to them, even if they themselves are externally the weaker ones and have to watch the debauchery defenselessly. Their bitter suffering, which goes as far as physical and mental breakdowns, is not in vain.[20] It is invisible martyrs' blood. It sprouts the seeds that grow in the winter night.

[20] One such breakdown Görres knew of was that of Father Hermann Breucha, her parish priest for many years and close friend in Stuttgart. In a letter, Görres writes: "Pastor Breucha, the poor good man, had a serious nervous breakdown last week *due to anguish about the Church*—first he cried day and night; now he is in the hospital. I can understand it, though I'm of tougher Japanese stock, thank God." Letter to Paulus Gordan, July 27, 1968, in *"Wirklich die neue Phönixgestalt?": Über Kirche und Konzil; Unbekannte Briefe 1962–1971 von Ida Friederike Görres an Paulus Gordan*, ed. Hanna-Barbara Gerl-Falkovitz (Heiligenkreuz im Wienerwald, Austria: Be+Be Verlag, 2015), 364. The controversial encyclical *Humanae vitae*, which Breucha defended, was released on July 25, 1968. In her introduction to Görres' book on Saint John Henry Newman, Hanna-Barbara Gerl-Falkovitz explains that Breucha "almost had a breakdown under the painful upheavals of 1968 and as well in

I believe in the *praying* Church, made up of laity and priests, the forbearing, the *atoning* Church. These are all terms that have become alien or ridiculous to many, yet they are the dormant powers among the people of Christendom. They are currently the anvil under the hammer, but their defenselessness is not a weakness. "What it takes to endure endless, recurring blows. The greatest force is only inward and used only as a counterpressure to ward off extreme unpleasantness", said Goethe somewhere.[21]

I believe in the hidden *saints*—there are certainly many—who participate today in Christ's concealment of Holy Saturday. Well, unfortunately, we see few of the impressive figures on which the weak faith would so much like to lean. Yet it seems that those who are called today are in the form not of the towering lighthouse shining into the distance but rather the heating system, sunk in the basement, unnoticed yet preserving life.

But I also believe that some visible messengers of God may be closer than we suspect. I believe in the many pure, good hearts among the youth who are concerned with what is real, who hunger and thirst for justice, who bide their time critically and are maturing gradually. God already knows them. He will call them at their hour. Did not Augustine say, when his church was almost empty because of a circus

---

regard to the discussion about *Humanae vitae*". (By Görres' account to Gordan, Breucha's breakdown was more serious than "almost".) Ida Friederike Görres, *John Henry Newman: A Life Sacrificed*, trans. Jennifer S. Bryson (San Francisco: Ignatius Press, 2024), 30.

[21] From a discussion between Johann Wolfgang von Goethe and Friedrich Wilhelm Riemer, April 1806. Johann Wolfgang von Goethe, *Goethes Gespräche (Anhang an Goethes Werke)*, ed. Woldemar Freiherr von Biedermann (Leipzig, Germany: F. W. von Biedermann, 1889–96), https://www.xn--gedichteundzitatefralle-tpc.de/2019/10/woldemar-von-biedermann-gesprache_3.html.

festival, "Who knows how many future bishops are now sitting in the stands at the circus and applauding the gladiators"?[22]

Maybe their grandchildren—out of generational contrariety!—will have had enough of trampling and rejection and will extract great discoveries from that which is defamed and withheld from them today.

They will receive the immortal seeds of life from the holy inheritance in their own way and, in their way, different from ours, will bear them to bring forth many fruits. Whether we older people experience this is really a matter of minor importance.

We must be satisfied with the knowledge that the City on the Hill is still there behind the fog that makes it invisible to many and that the enemies can often smash only the backdrop sets and artificial images. We must be able to wait through snowmelt and flood and even starless nights, knowing that stars are more enduring than clouds. What is up to us is to plead without ceasing for discernment and love, for justice and patience—and for unshakable *love* for the Church. Because only the lover discerns. And what people who do not love her, maybe secretly hate her, tell us about her need not frighten us. But we also have to pray for the inner freedom to let go of much that is beloved and precious

[22] Görres paraphrases Saint Augustine, who mentions such a scenario twice. Her paraphrase is most similar to his exposition of Psalm 147. Augustine, *Expositions of the Psalms*, vol. 3, *Psalms 121–150*, trans. Maria Boulding, ed. Boniface Ramsey (Hyde Park, N.Y.: New City Press, 2000), 526–27, 522. Also, in book 6 of his *Confessions*, Augustine tells about his friend Alypius, who used to squander time at the "futile entertainments" and "games in the amphitheatre" in Carthage; later, to the surprise of Saint Augustine, Alypius became a Catholic priest and eventually bishop of Thagaste. Saint Augustine, *Confessions*, trans. R. S. Pine-Coffin (New York: Penguin Books, 1961), 120–21.

to us if doing so is really necessary for the renovation and peace of the city of God, because God takes away not only bad and worthless things but very often also precious things.

> You're the one, who, whatever we mold
> shatters it upon us, you, clement,
> So that Heaven we behold.
> Thus, I shall not lament.[23]
>
> —Eichendorff

We must always pray from now on for the *courage* to defend what has been entrusted to us, tenaciously, bravely, stubbornly, and at all costs to defend that which is holy—because, even in worldly history, those wonderful rescues and victories did not happen to the cowardly and idle but truly only to those engaged in the highest or lowest moments of struggle. This courage must grow together with darkness and threat. A great saying has come down to us from King Alfred of England, a contemporary of Charlemagne, who said, under the Danish onslaught, when the barbarians flooded his homeland and forced him back into the last free corner:

"Tougher the spirit, bolder the hearts, stronger the courage when power diminishes!"[24] And I wholeheartedly believe in the theology of moon symbolism, the strangely prophetic

[23] Joseph Freiherr von Eichendorff, "Der Umkehrende", in *Ausgewählte Werke: Gedichte*, ed. Hans A. Neunzig (Munich: Nymphenburger, 1987), 278. Translation by Bryson.

[24] Görres appears to be paraphrasing a passage from section 3 of King Alfred the Great's translation of Gregory the Great's *On Pastoral Care*. *Alfred the Great: Asser's Life of King Alfred and Other Contemporary Sources*, trans. Michael Lapidge and Simon Keynes (London: Penguin Books, 2004), 127–28. Görres loved English history and culture. At the University of Freiburg, she wrote a university thesis (though did not complete her degree) on King Edmund (d. 869), also known as Saint Edmund the Martyr.

theology of Origen, which Hugo Rahner has once again made accessible to us: The Church is the moon, the splendor of which is tarnished by our sins and fades to seemingly total darkness. But in the darkest hour, Christ, the Sun, touches her anew and fills her again with increasing light.

APPENDIX

Eulogy for Ida Friederike Görres

Joseph Ratzinger
Requiem Mass, Cathedral of Freiburg, Germany
May 19, 1971

The Church engages in worship by commemorating the death of her Lord. She does this gratefully because she knows that this death has given life to suffering. With such knowledge, the Church dares to give thanks at the graves of her dead. She can do this because she believes that the death of those who believe in Jesus Christ is held in His death and thus in His Resurrection. It is overcome in advance. It is not destruction but merely transition into a new and final way of being with God and with all who belong to the Lord.

Nevertheless, humanly speaking, this is something shocking, and sometimes we feel this outrageousness, such as when the words from the Song of Zechariah, which had been a song at the birth of a long-awaited child, are used at

This is a translation of Joseph Ratzinger, "Gedenkworte zum Heimgang von Ida Friederike Görres," in *Aus meinem Leben: Autobiographische Texte*, edited by Gerhard Ludwig Müller, 15, Joseph Ratzinger Gesammelte Schriften (Freiburg im Breisgau: Herder, 2022). This eulogy also appeared as Joseph Ratzinger, "Gedenkworte zum Heimgang von Ida Friederike Görres", in Ida Görres, Walter Nigg, and Joseph Ratzinger, *Aufbruch—aber keine Auflösung: Briefe über die Kirche und anderes*, ed. Beatrix Klaiber (Freiburg im Breisgau: Jung Verlag, 1971), 145–51. This translation was published previously as Joseph Ratzinger, "Eulogy for Ida Friederike Görres", trans. Jennifer S. Bryson, *Logos* 23, no. 4 (September 9, 2020): 148–55. It has been edited lightly for this book.

the open grave: "Blessed be the Lord God of Israel, for he has visited and redeemed his people."[1] In the face of tears and pain, in the face of all the hardship and abandonment that a person's departure can mean, the Church praises God and sees in this fate of death His visitation, His closeness that gives salvation. And even before that, in the center of the liturgy, the words ring out: "It is truly right and just, our duty and our salvation, always and everywhere to give You thanks"—even at this hour.

Even at this hour: Can we give thanks? Can we give thanks at the death of Ida Friederike Görres, with which a voice has been taken away from us, a voice that seems irreplaceable to the Church in this situation, when we are in a desert of conformism or embarrassed silence? She spoke with an insightful certainty and a fearlessness about the pressing questions and tasks of the Church today, something that given only to the one who truly believes. And where else are there such voices?

Yet all of this was not merely a matter of course for her. She had grown up in the liberal Catholicism of the waning Habsburg monarchy. Her education at a convent provided access to faith, rooted her in it, but everything remained strangely stale, inanimate, dry. What brought the great turning point was encountering the [Catholic] Youth Movement, which determined her entire further path until the end. She realized what, from then on, remained the center of her thought and work: the living Church. She realized that the Church is not just an organization, a hierarchy, an administrative office but an organism that grows and lives through the centuries. She realized that the Church is not just the small spatial and temporal segment to which we belong, the

[1] Lk 1:68.

whole community of believers throughout all eras but all locations belongs to the Church "until today, fulfilling her history from century to century, growing, unfolding, struggling, ailing, recovering, living out her destiny and maturing toward the return of the Lord".[2] This very community throughout the eras, the whole that lives from the Lord—this is the Church in which the Lord Himself continues to walk through time and to draw her to Himself.

From this vantage point, a decisive insight had become for her a self-evident matter that, at the same time, made it possible for her to survive the periods of blackout in the past few years and to maintain independence and serenity in them: a church built in this way must be the Church of sinners. In her last letter to me, she supported this idea passionately: A church of the elites—what would that be? No, it is precisely this that belongs to the Church: that she reaches down to the lowest wretchedness of man, is disfigured by it, wounded, often almost completely concealed. Still, however, this permeates everything again and again, that she calls all illness her own and, in this way, brings this to the Lord, who desired to take on our weakness.

Certainly, it was not easy at the same time for Ida Friederike Görres to deal with a Church that no longer seemed to know herself and often appeared to be her own opponent. One of her most recent presentations, her speech "Trusting the Church?",[3] gives us a rousing insight into her questions and struggles with what was becoming an ever-new necessity of groping one's way along in the Church:

[2] "Trusting the Church", p. 162.

[3] This question mark in the title "Trusting the Church?" appears only in the 1971 version of the Ratzinger eulogy. In the 1970 printed edition of the Görres lecture, "Vertrauen zur Kirche" [Trusting the Church], there is no question mark in the title of the lecture.

> What if the rebels really were to own the future? What if this process, which seems to us like destruction and betrayal, were actually God's Will and to resist it were impious and an act of petty faith? What if—an agonizing thought in the midnight hours—what if I were tied to a great but inexorably dying body, through merely emotionally stirring but ultimately subjective, unreasonable inhibitions, habits, prejudices, antiquated piety, wrongly grounded loyalty? . . . Are we living on a leaky ship sinking inch by inch, from which not only the rats but also the sensible, sober people jump off just in time?[4]

But all this questioning is offset by a great, indestructible confidence. It is expressed in the simple yet likewise great affirmation: "I believe in God's faithfulness."[5] From this center, she was able to survive during the crisis of this mysterious organism, even to advance during the crisis and grow to a deeper understanding. I believe in God's faithfulness—this statement is followed by what is almost a hymn of confidence, hope, and joy: "I trust the suffering in the Church. . . . I believe in the praying Church, made up of laity and priests, the forbearing, the atoning Church." "I believe in the hidden saints."[6] She, who had been ill for a long time, belonged, to a great extent, to the suffering and the praying Church, to that living center, which is the assurance for all of us. And in all of this, there was no fanaticism, no rigidity in her. It was especially in the loyalty that imbued her life that she stayed lively, kept going. Until the very end, she emanated an unrestrained cheerfulness that is possible only for a person who knows herself to be in harmony with the Truth.

[4] "Trusting the Church", pp. 161–62.

[5] "Trusting the Church", p. 176.

[6] "Trusting the Church", pp. 178, 179.

And so we ask again: Can we be thankful at this death? I think we can and must say yes. We thank God that she existed, that this insightful, brave, faithful woman was given to the Church in this century. We give thanks for her writing, for the way she was and will continue to be present to many people through her writing. We give thanks for the path along which God led her, step by step. And we give thanks for the death that He gave her: she was called from the midst of her witness, from her work on the synod commission.[7] She had been invited by friends to vacation in Styria, but ministry was more important to her—no matter how much she had been looking forward to pleasant days in her beloved Austria. We can give thanks—most deeply because we know that she has not been taken from us but only changed her location, as it were, in the communion of saints, in that living Church spanning across all time and borders, in which she believed and for which she lived.

She followed a path to the end, whose goal for her was hope. In the lecture that I mentioned, there is the witness of this hope of hers: "The new taboos are also good for something; rarely heard words unfold their almost unbearable force again"; I am on the way "to eternal bliss in the perfect unity of God, in the physical resurrection in a New Heaven and a New Earth".[8] I am on the way to eternal bliss—for her, that was not a figure of speech but calm certainty. I am on the way to eternal bliss: at this hour, we want to ask God to say His definitive yes to such faith. Amen.

[7] Ida Görres served on a commission of the Synod of Würzburg. On May 14, 1971, she collapsed after giving a passionate speech at the synod—as Ratzinger says, "called from the midst of her witness"; she died the next day in hospital in Frankfurt.

[8] "Trusting the Church", p. 164.

Register of Persons

Unless otherwise identified, the priests, bishops, cardinals, and saints in this register of persons are Roman Catholic.

Albertus Magnus (ca. 1200–1280): saint, Dominican priest, and scholar.

Alfred the Great (848 or 849–899): king of the Anglo-Saxons.

Alypius of Thagaste (fourth to fifth century): convert, bishop, and friend of Saint Augustine mentioned in his *Confessions*.

Anselm of Canterbury (1033 or 1034–1109): saint, monk, philosopher, theologian, and archbishop.

Asch, Sholem (1880–1957): Polish Jewish novelist (also spelled Shalom and Schalom).

Ascher, Jaakow Jizchak ben (1766–1813): Hasidic rabbi in Przysucha, Poland.

Asmussen, Hans (1898–1968): Lutheran pastor and friend of Ida Görres.

Augustine of Hippo (354–430): saint, bishop.

Ball, Hugo (1886–1927): German author and founder of the Dada movement.

Benda, Julien (1867–1956), French philosopher, novelist, and cultural critic.

Benedict XVI (1927–2022): né Joseph Ratzinger, German priest, cardinal, pope (2005–2013), pope emeritus (2013–

2022); corresponded with Ida Görres and gave the eulogy at her funeral (see appendix).

Benedict of Nursia (480–547): saint, founder of monasteries, and author of *The Rule of Saint Benedict.*

Bergengruen, Werner (1892–1964): Baltic-German novelist, poet, and Catholic convert.

Bernanos, Georges (1888–1948): French Catholic novelist.

Bernard of Clairvaux (1090–1153): saint, monk, revitalizer of monasticism, and Doctor of the Church.

Brentano, Clemens (1778–1842): Romantic-era German poet and novelist.

Breucha, Hermann (1902–1972): parish priest of Ida and Carl-Josef Görres in Degerloch-Stuttgart and friend of Ida Görres.

Buber, Martin (1878–1965): Austrian Jewish philosopher and translator of the Hebrew Bible into German.

Câmara, Hélder (1909–1999): Brazilian priest and archbishop of Olinda and Recife (1964–1985).

Catherine of Siena (1347–1380): saint, lay Dominican, mystic, author, and Doctor of the Church.

Cénabre, Abbé: in the novel *Under the Sun of Satan* by Georges Bernanos, a priest who is an atheist studying mysticism.

Charlemagne (747–814): king of the Franks and the Lombards and Holy Roman emperor (800–814).

Christopher (third or fourth century): saint and martyr.

Chrysostom, John (ca. 347–407): saint, bishop, and Doctor of the Church.

Claudius, Matthias (1740–1815): German poet.

Defoe, Daniel (ca. 1660–1731): English writer and author of *Robinson Crusoe.*

Dessauer, Philipp (1898–1966): German priest and theologian.

De Foucauld, Charles (1858–1916): saint, French soldier, priest, and hermit.

Eichendorff, Joseph Freiherr von (1788–1857): German poet, novelist, and playwright.

Emmerich, Anne Catherine (1774–1824): blessed, Augustinian Canoness Regular of Windesheim, mystic, and visionary.

Faulhaber, Michael von (1869–1952): German priest, cardinal, and bishop of Munich and Freising (1917–1952).

Francis of Assisi (1182–1226): saint and founder of the Franciscan Order.

Fugel, Gebhard (1863–1939): German painter of Christian motifs.

Goethe, Johann Wolfgang von (1749–1832): German poet, playwright, novelist, and scholar.

Gordan, Paulus, O.S.B. (1912–1999): German Catholic convert from Judaism, priest, monk at the monastery of Beuron, and friend and correspondent of Ida Görres.

Görres, Albert (1918–1996): psychologist and brother-in-law of Ida Görres.

Guardini, Romano (1885–1968): German priest and leading figure in the Catholic Youth Movement, in which Görres played an active role.

Haecker, Theodor (1879–1945): German Catholic convert and translator of John Henry Newman.

Heer, Friedrich (1916–1983): Austrian historian; *see also* Nicodemus.

Hensel, Luise (1798–1876): German Protestant poet.

Ignatius of Loyola (1491–1556): saint and founder of the Society of Jesus.

Innocent III (1160 or 1161–1216): né Lotario dei Conti di Segni, pope (1198–1216).

John XXIII (1881–1863): né Angelo Giuseppe Roncalli, saint, pope (1958–1963).

John Paul II (1920–2005): né Karol Józef Wojtyła, saint, pope (1978–2005).

Jung, Carl Gustav (1875–1961): Swiss psychiatrist and psychoanalyst.

Jünger, Ernst (1895–1998): German soldier and author.

Küng, Hans (1928–2021): Swiss priest, theologian on the faculty at the University of Tübingen; from 1978 on, the Catholic Church denied him permission to teach Catholic theology due to his nonorthodox views.

Läpple, Alfred (1915–2013): German priest and colleague of Joseph Ratzinger.

Lewis, C. S. (1898–1963): English author and Anglican; Görres admired Lewis' work and translated some of his essays into German.

Lorenz, Konrad (1903–1989): Austrian zoologist and researcher of animal behavior.

Luther, Martin (1483–1546): German Protestant theologian and key figure in the Protestant Reformation.

Marinetti, Filippo Tommaso (1876–1944): Italian founder of the Futurist movement and author of the *Futurist Manifesto*.

Mary (d. first century): saint and Mother of Jesus.

Möhler, Johann Adam (1796–1838): German theologian and Church historian.

More, Thomas (1478–1535): saint, martyr, and English lawyer and judge.

Newman, John Henry (1801–1890): English Catholic convert and cardinal (1879–1890); Görres wrote a biography of him. (See Görres, *John Henry Newman* in the bibliography, under German works.)

Nicodemus (d. first century): saint, Pharisee, and member of the Sanhedrin mentioned in the Gospel of John (3:1–2).

Nigg, Walter (1903–1988): Swiss Reformed theologian and scholar of the lives of saints.

Origen (ca. 185–ca. 253): early Christian scholar and Church Father.

Ortega y Gasset, José (1883–1955): Spanish philosopher and essayist.

Pascal, Blaise (1623–1662): French Catholic philosopher and theologian.

Paul VI (1897–1978): né Giovanni Battista Enrico Antonio Maria Montini, saint, pope (1963–1978).

Rahner, Hugo (1900–1968): German Jesuit priest and theologian.

Rahner, Karl (1904–1984): German Jesuit priest and theologian.

Ratzinger, Joseph. *See* Pope Benedict XVI.

Riemer, Friedrich Wilhelm (1774–1845): German scholar and literary historian; assistant to Johann Wolfgang von Goethe.

Robinson Crusoe: a character in the eponymous book.

Robinson, John A. T. (1919–1983): Anglican bishop and New Testament scholar.

Rosenstock-Huessy, Eugen (1888–1973): German Jewish historian, social philosopher, and convert to Lutheranism.

Saul of Tarsus (ca. 5–ca. 64 or 65): saint; Paul the Apostle.

Sayers, Dorothy (1893–1957): English author and poet.

Schulmeister, Otto (1916–2001): Austrian journalist and editor, affiliated with the journal *Wort und Wahrheit* (1947–1968) and the newspaper *Die Presse* (1946–1989).

Schurr, Viktor (1898–1971): German Redemptorist priest.

Seewald, Peter (b. 1954): German journalist and author of a biography of Joseph Ratzinger/Pope Benedict XVI.

Stephen (5–34): saint, first martyr.

Stern, Karl (1906–1975): German Jewish convert to Catholicism, neurologist, and psychiatrist; later lived in Canada.

Talleyrand-Périgord, Charles-Maurice de (1754–1838), French priest and statesman.

Teilhard de Chardin, Pierre (1881–1955): French Jesuit priest, paleontologist, and theologian.

Teresa of Calcutta (1910–1997): saint and founder of the Missionaries of Charity; known as Mother Teresa; Görres mentions having contact with her after the Second Vatican Council.

Thérèse of Lisieux (1873–1897): saint and French Carmelite nun; Görres' biography of her is Görres' most well-known work. (See Görres, *The Hidden Face* in the bibliography, under English works.)

Thorvaldsen, Bertel (1770–1844): Danish sculptor.

Volk, Georg (1898–1986): German medical doctor and author.

Von Balthasar, Hans Urs (1905–1988): Swiss priest, theologian; corresponded with Ida Görres.

Von Speyr, Adrienne (1902–1967): Swiss convert, mystic, and close associate of Hans Urs von Balthasar.

Von Hügel, Friedrich (1852–1925): Austrian author.

Werfel, Franz (1890–1945): Austrian Bohemian novelist.

Wojtyła, Karol. *See* John Paul II.

Bibliography

In English

Alfred the Great: Asser's Life of King Alfred and Other Contemporary Sources. Translated by Michael Lapidge, Simon Keynes. London: Penguin Books, 2004.

Augustine, Saint. *Confessions*. Translated by R. S. Pine-Coffin. New York: Penguin Books, 1961.

———. *Expositions of the Psalms, 121–150*, trans. Maria Boulding, The Works of Saint Augustine, ed. Boniface Ramsey, III/20. Hyde Park, N.Y.: New City Press, 2000.

Benda, Julien. *The Betrayal of the Intellectuals*. Translated by Richard Aldington. Boston: Beacon Press, 1969.

Bernanos, Georges. *Under the Sun of Satan*. Translated by Harry Lorin Binsse. Providence: Cluny Media, 2017.

Bryson, Jennifer Sue. "Ida Friederike Görres in Translation 1932–2022: A Bibliography in Fifteen Languages". In *"Glut und Schmerz des Glaubens": Ein neuer Blick auf Ida Friederike Görres (1901–1971)*, edited by Sigmund Bonk. Regensburg: Verlag Friedrich Pustet, 2023.

———. "The Reception of Ida Friederike Görres in English from 1932 to 2022". In Bonk, *"Glut und Schmerz des Glaubens"*.

Bryson, Jennifer S. Translator's note. In Görres, *The Church in the Flesh*. Providence: Cluny Media, 2023.

Bryson, Jennifer S. "Why Do Heretics Remain in the Church?" *Crisis Magazine*, March 24, 2023. https://crisismagazine.com/opinion/why-do-heretics-remain-in-the-church.

Câmara, Hélder. *Helder Camara*. Ladoc "Keyhole" Series 12. Washington, D.C.: Latin America Documentation, 1975.

Coudenhove, Ida Friederike. *The Burden of Belief.* With an introduction by Gerald Vann. Translated by Conrad Mario Ricco Bonacina. London: Sheed and Ward, 1934.

———. *The Cloister and the World.* Translated by Harriette Eleanor Kennedy. London: Sheed and Ward, 1935.

———. "The Nature of Sanctity: A Dialogue". In *The Persistence of Order: Essays on Religion and Culture*, edited by T. F. Burns and Christopher Dawson, translated by Ruth Bonsall and Edward Watkin, 1:125–96. Providence: Cluny Media, 2019.

Eichendorff, Joseph Freiherr von. "Der Umkehrende". In *Ausgewählte Werke: Gedichte*, edited by Hans A. Neunzig, 277–79. Munich: Nymphenburger, 1987.

Goethe, Johann Wolfgang von. *Faust: First Part / Faust: Erster Teil.* Translated by Peter Salm. A Bantam Dual-Language Book. New York: Bantam, 1962.

———. "The God and the Bayadere". In *Goethe*, translated by John Whaley, 48–50. London: Everyman, 2000.

Görres, Ida Friederike. *The Church in the Flesh.* Translated by Jennifer Sue Bryson. Providence: Cluny Media, 2023.

———. *The Hidden Face: A Study of Saint Thérèse of Lisieux.* Translated by Richard and Clara Winston. San Francisco: Ignatius Press, 2003.

———. *Is Celibacy Outdated?* Translated by Barbara Waldstein-Wartenberg. Westminster, Md.: Newman Press, 1965.

———. "A Letter on the Church". Translated by Ida Friederike Görres. *Dublin Review* 223, no. 446 (Winter 1949): 71–89.

———. *Mary Ward.* Translated by Elise Codd. London: Longmans, Green, 1939.

———. *On Marriage and on Being Single.* Translated by Jennifer S. Bryson. (Forthcoming).

———. "Trusting the Church: A Lecture". Translated by Jennifer S. Bryson. *Logos* 23, no. 4 (September 9, 2020): 123–47.

———. "Trusting the Church: A Lecture". Translated by Jennifer S. Bryson. Read by Karina Majewski. Catholic Culture Audiobooks. Podcast audio. June 15, 2021. https://www.catholicculture.org/commentary/ida-friederike-grres-trusting-church/.

———. *What Binds Marriage Forever.* Introduction by Jonathan Bieler. Translated by Jennifer S. Bryson. Washington, D.C.: Catholic University of America Press, 2025.

———. "When Does a Person Have a Capacity for Liturgy?" Translated by Jennifer S. Bryson. *Logos* 25, no. 3 (Summer 2022): 126–39.

Gregory XVI. *Mirari vos.* Encyclical letter, August 15, 1832.

Guitton, Jean. *The Church and the Laity: From Newman to Vatican II.* Translated by Malachy Gerard Carroll. Staten Island, N.Y.: Alba House, 1965.

Heer, Friedrich. *The Medieval World: Europe, 1100–1350*. London: Weidenfeld and Nicolson, 1993.

Hoger Katechetisch Instituut, Nijmegen (Netherlands). *A New Catechism: Catholic Faith for Adults*. Translated by Kevin Smyth. New York: Herder and Herder, 1972.

Ignatius of Loyola. *The Spiritual Exercises of St. Ignatius of Loyola*. Translated by Elder Mullan. New York: P.J. Kenedy and Sons, 1914.

Jünger, Ernst. *The Worker: Dominion and Form*. Edited by Laurence Paul Hemming. Translated by Laurence Paul Hemming and Bogdan Costea. Evanston, Ill.: Northwestern University Press, 2017.

Lewis, C.S. *The Collected Letters of C.S. Lewis*. Vol. 11. Edited by Walter Hooper. San Francisco: HarperSanFrancisco, 2004.

———. *Letters to Malcolm: Chiefly on Prayer*. New York: Harcourt, Brace and World, 1964.

———. "Modern Theology and Biblical Criticism". In *Christian Reflections*, edited by Walter Hooper, 187–205. Grand Rapids: William B. Eerdmans, 1967.

Marinetti, Filippo Tommaso. "The Founding and Manifesto of Futurism". In *Marinetti's Selected Writings*, translated by R.W. Flint, 19–24. New York: Farrar, Straus and Giroux, 1972.

Möhler, Johann Adam. *Unity in the Church, or, The Principle of Catholicism: Presented in the Spirit of the Church Fathers of the First Three Centuries*. Translated by Peter C. Erb. Washington, D.C.: Catholic University of America Press, 2016.

Newman, John Henry. *An Essay on the Development of Christian Doctrine*. London: Longmans, Green, 1909.

———. "On Consulting the Faithful in Matters of Doctrine". *Rambler*, July 1859. https://newmanreader.org/works/rambler/consulting.html.

———. "Sermon 1. The Philosophical Temper, First Enjoined by the Gospel". In *Fifteen Sermons Preached before the University of Oxford*, 1–15. London: Longmans, Green, 1909. https://www.newmanreader.org/works/oxford/sermon1.html.

Nietzsche, Friedrich. *The Gay Science*. Translated by Walter Kaufmann. New York: Vintage Books, 1974.

———. *Thus Spoke Zarathustra: A Book for All and None*. Translated by Walter Kaufmann. New York: Penguin Books, 1978.

Ortega y Gasset, José. *The Revolt of the Masses*. New York: W. W. Norton and Company, 1932. https://archive.org/details/revoltofmasses0000unse/page/n1/mode/2up.

Paul VI. Encyclical letter *Humanae vitae*. July 25, 1968.

———. Apostolic letter *Solemni hac liturgia* [Credo of the People of God]. June 30, 1968.

Pius XII. Encyclical *Humani generis*. August 12, 1950.

Rahner, Karl. "The Parish Priest". In *Mission and Grace: Essays in Pastoral Theology*, vol. 2, translated by Cecily Hastings and Richard Strachan, 35–52. London: Sheed and Ward, 1963.

Ratzinger, Joseph. "Eulogy for Ida Friederike Görres". Translated by Jennifer S. Bryson. *Logos* 23, no. 4 (September 9, 2020): 148–55.

———. *God and the World: A Conversation with Peter Seewald.* Translated by Henry Taylor. San Francisco: Ignatius Press, 2002.

Rosenberg, Alfons. "A Panoramic View of Ida Friederike Görres," in Görres, *The Church in the Flesh*, xiii–xxv.

Sayers, Dorothy. *The Man Born to Be King: A Play-Cycle on the Life of Our Lord Jesus Christ.* London: Victor Gollancz, 1943.

Schmöger, K. E. *The Life of Anne Catherine Emmerich.* Vol. 1. Rockford, Ill.: TAN Books, 1976.

Seewald, Peter. *Benedict XVI: A Life.* Vol. 1, *Youth in Nazi Germany to the Second Vatican Council 1927–1965.* Translated by Dinah Livingstone. London: Bloomsbury Continuum, 2020.

Six, Jean-François. *Witness in the Desert: The Life of Charles de Foucauld.* Translated by Lucie Noel. New York: Macmillan, 1965.

Stern, Karl. *The Flight from Woman.* New York: Farrar, Straus and Giroux, 1965.

Teilhard de Chardin, Pierre. "The Evolution of Chastity". In *Toward the Future*, translated by René Hague, 60–86. New York: Harcourt Brace Jovanovich, 1975.

Wegemer, Gerard B. *Thomas More: A Portrait of Courage.* New York: Scepter Publishers, 1995.

Werfel, Franz. *Hearken unto the Voice*. Translated by Moray Firth. London: Jarrolds, 1938.

Zagorin, Perez. *Ways of Lying: Dissimulation, Persecution, and Conformity in Early Modern Europe*. Cambridge, Mass.: Harvard University Press, 1990.

In German

Asmussen, Hans. *Das Geheimnis der Liebe*. Stuttgart, Germany: Evangelisches Verlagswerk, 1962.

Ball, Hugo. *Byzantinisches Christentum: Drei Heiligenleben (zu Joannes Klimax, Dionysius Areopagita und Symeon dem Styliten)*. Einsiedeln, Switzerland: Benziger Verlag, 1958.

Braun, Karl-Heinz. "'Seine Zelibatspolemik wird ihm keine Rosen bringen . . .' Zum Freiburger Moraltheologen Heinrich Schreiber und seinen Kollegen in der Theologischen Fakultät." *Zeitschrift des Breisgau-Geschichtsvereins Schau-ins-Land*, no. 116, 1997: 207–225.

Bryson, Jennifer Sue. "Eine unabsehbare Wechselwirkung von menschlicher und göttlicher Liebe: "'Die Braut des Alexis' von Ida Friederike Görres." In *Neue Schau: Große Erzählungen im 20. Jahrhundert*. Edited by Hanna-Barbara Gerl-Falkovitz and Gudrun Trausmuth, vol. 9, 191–98. Kleine Bibliothek des Abendlandes. Heiligenkreuz im Wienerwald, Austria: Be+Be-Verlag, 2023.

Claudius, Matthias. "An seinen Sohn". In *The Oxford Book of German Prose / Das Oxforder Buch Deutscher Prosa: Von Luther bis Rilke*, 120–23. Edited by H. G. Fiedler. Oxford, U.K.: Oxford University Press, 1943.

Coudenhove, Ida Friederike. *The Burden of Belief. With an Introduction by Gerald Vann, O.P.* Translated by Conrad Mario Ricco Bonacina. London: Sheed & Ward, 1934.

———. "The Nature of Sanctity: A Dialogue." In *Essays on Religion and Culture*, edited by T. F. Burns Christopher Dawson, translated by Ruth Bonsall and Edward Watkin, 1:125–96. The Persistence of Order. Providence: Cluny Media, 2019.

Fugel, Gebhard. *Biblische Schulwandbilder.* Munich: Ars Sacra, J. Mueller, 1931–1939.

Goethe, Johann Wolfgang von. *Goethes Gespräche (Anhang an Goethes Werke).* Edited by Freiherr Woldemar von Biedermann. Leipzig, Germany: F. W. von Biedermann, 1889–96. https://www.xn--gedichteundzitatefralle-tpc.de/2019/10/woldemar-von-biedermann-gesprache_3.html.

Görres, Albert. "Psychologische Bemerkungen zur Krise eines Berufsstandes". In *Weltpriester nach dem Konzil*, Münchener Akademie-Schriften, vol. 46, edited by Franz Heinrich, 119–41. Munich: Kösel Verlag, 1969.

Görres, Ida Friederike. "Abbruchkommandos in der Kirche: Der Katholizismus zwischen den Kräften der Zerstörung und der Rodung für eine neue Zeit". *Die Presse*, Weekend Supplement, March 29–30, 1969.

———. *Des andern Last: ein Gespräch über die Barmherzigkeit.* Herder, 1940.

———. *Be-Denkliches: Über die Mischehe und anderes Zeitgespräch.* Donauwörth, Germany: Verlag Ludwig Auer, 1966.

———. "Bemerkungen zum Zölibatstreit", *Die Sendung* 23 (1970): 17–21.

———. "Bemerkungen zum Zölibat", *Unphilosophische Brocken* 4 (1969).

———. "Eine Besinnung über die Spiritualität des Theologie-Studiums". In *Wort in Welt: Studien zur Theologie der Verkündigung; Festgabe für Viktor Schurr*, edited by Wolfdieter Theurer, 272–284. Bergen-Enkheim bei Frankfurt am Main: Kaffke, 1968.

———. "Die Braut des Alexis". In *Die Braut des Alexis und andere Mädchengeschichten*, 261–93. Freiburg im Breisgau: Herder, 1949. [English translation by Bryson forthcoming.]

———. "Brief über die Kirche". *Frankfurter Hefte* 1, no. 8 (1946): 715–33.

———. "'Engel und Teufel sind abgeschafft': Noch Vertrauen zur Kirche?" *Die Furche*, June 19, 1971, 10.

———. "Flucht vor der 'Mutter' Kirche," *Rheinischer Merkur*, July 11, 1969.

———. "Geleitwort". Thomas Gilby. *Kleiner Kompaß für Eheleute*, 7–12. Translated by Elisabeth Maurer. Freiburg im Breisgau: Herder, 1956.

———. "Das Gespräch über die Kirche [Aufsatz II]". *Frankfurter Hefte* 2, no. 3 (1947): 279–84.

———. *Laiengedanken zum Zölibat*. Frankfurt am Main, Germany: Knecht Verlag, 1962.

———. "Überbetonung des Maskulinen drängt in der Kirche Flucht vor der 'Mutter' Kirche," *Die Furche*, nr. 32 (August 9, 1969): 9.

———. *Im Winter wächst das Brot: Sechs Versuche über die Kirche.* Einsiedeln, Switzerland: Johannes Verlag, 1970.

———. "Laie und Kirche". *Der Christliche Sonntag* (June 19, 1960).

———. "Maria war damals die ganze Kirche". *Freiburger Artikel- und Redaktionsdienst* 12, no. 18 (February 22, 1968): 2–3.

———. "Neues über die Liebe?" Review of *Neues über die Liebe?*, by Hans Asmussen. *Der christliche Sonntag* 15, no. 30 (1963): 237–38.

———. "Die Schatzhöhle: Ein Geleitwort". In Alfons Rosenberg. *Michael und der Drache: Urgestalten von Licht und Finsternis*, 7–12. Olten, Germany: Walter Verlag, 1956. [English translation by Jennifer Sue Bryson unpublished.]

———. *Von Ehe und von Einsamkeit: Ein Beitrag in vier Briefen.* Donauwörth, Germany: Cassianeum, 1949.

———. *"Wirklich die neue Phönixgestalt?": Über Kirche und Konzil; Unbekannte Briefe 1962–1971 von Ida Friederike Görres an Paulus Gordan*. Edited by Hanna-Barbara Gerl-Falkovitz. Heiligenkreuz im Wienerwald, Austria: Be+Be Verlag, 2015.

———. "Zu unserem Christus Bild: Ein Brief". In *Unphilosophische Brocken* 2 (1968).

Görres, Ida Friederike. Excerpt from "Zu unserem Christusbild", in *Jesus 2000 Jahre Glaubens- und Kulturgeschichte*. Freiburg im Breisgau: Herder, 1999.

Görres, Ida Friederike, and Joseph Ratzinger. "Fragen eines Laien zur theologischen Diskussion über das priesterliche Amt aus einem Briefwechsel zwischen Ida Friederike Görres und Joseph Ratzinger". *Geist und Leben: Zeitschrift für Aszese und Mystik* 42, no. 3 (June 1969): 220–24.

Guardini, Romano. "Anselm von Canterbury und das Wesen der Theologie." In *Auf dem Wege*. Mainz: Matthias-Grünewald-Verlag, 1923.

———. "Das Erwachen der Kirche in der Seele". *Hochland* 19 (1922): 257–67.

Guitton, Jean. *Mitbürgen der Wahrheit: Das Zeugnis der Laien in Fragen der Glaubenslehre*. Translated by Ludwig Fabritius. Salzburg: Otto Müller Verlag, 1964.

Hensel, Luise, "Jesus in der Heiligen Schrift". In Winfried Freund. *Müde bin ich, geh' zur Ruh: Leben und Werk der Luise Hensel*, 81–82. Wiedenbrück, Germany: Güth + Etscheidt, 1984.

Kleinert, Michael. *Es wächst viel Brot in der Winternacht: Theologische Grundlinien im Werk von Ida Friederike Görres*. Vol. 36 of Studien zur systematischen und spirituellen Theologie. Würzburg: Echter, 2002.

Lewis, C. S. "Moderne Theologie und Bibelkritik: Ein Vortrag". Translated by Ida Friederike Görres. *Erbe und Auftrag* 44, no. 4 (1968): 291–302.

Möhler, Johann Adam. *Kirche und Geschichte*. Edited by Bernhard Hanssler. Vol. 33 of Zeugen des Wortes. Freiburg im Breisgau: Herder, 1941.

Rahner, Karl. "Die ewige Bedeutung der Menschheit Jesu für unser Gottesverhältnis". In *Menschsein und Menschwerdung Gottes: Studien zur Grundlegung der Dogmatik, zur Christologie, Theologischen Anthropologie und Eschatologie*, edited by H. Vorgrimler, Sämtliche Werke, vol. 12, 251–60. Freiburg im Breisgau: Herder, 2005.

Ratzinger, Joseph. "Eulogy for Ida Friederike Görres". Translated by Jennifer S. Bryson. *Logos* 23, no. 4 (September 9, 2020): 148–55.

———. "Gedenkworte zum Heimgang von Ida Friederike Görres" . In *Aus meinem Leben: Autobiographische Texte*, edited by Gerhard Ludwig Müller. Vol. 15 of Joseph Ratzinger Gesammelte Schriften. Freiburg im Breisgau, Germany: Herder, forthcoming.

———. "Gedenkworte zum Heimgang von Ida Friederike Görres". In *Aus meinem Leben: Autobiographische Texte*, edited by Gerhard Ludwig Müller. Vol. 15 of Joseph Ratzinger Gesammelte Schriften. Freiburg im Breisgau, Germany: Herder, forthcoming.

———. "Gedenkworte zum Heimgang von Ida Friederike Görres." In *Aufbruch—aber keine Auflösung: Briefe über die Kirche und anderes*, by Ida Görres, Walter Nigg, and Joseph Ratzinger, edited by Beatrix Klaiber, 145–51. Freiburg im Breisgau, Germany: Jung Verlag, 1971.

Rosenberg, Alfons, ed. *Wanderwege. Festschrift zum 60: Geburtstag von Ida Friederike Görres*. Zurich: Thomas Verlag, 1961.

Scharrelmann, Wilhelm. *Jesus der Jüngling*. Leipzig, Germany: Quelle and Meyer, 1925.

In Other Languages

Görres, Ida Friederike. "Från celibat till äktenskap?" *Credo* 51, no. 1 (1970): 9–14.

Note: regarding the following entries in Hungarian, Dutch, Polish, and Slovenian. I do not know the title of Görres' essay in each language nor the page numbers in each translation.

Görres, Ida Friederike. Excerpt from "Our Image of Christ", in *Jézus: 2000 éves hit-és kultúrtörténet*. Szeged, Hungary: Agapé, 2000.

———. Excerpt from "Our Image of Christ", *Jezus: 2000 jaar geloofs- en cultuurgeschiedenis*. Baarn, Netherlands: Tirion, 2000.

———. Excerpt from "Our Image of Christ", *Jezus: 2000 Lat Obecności*. Kraków: Wydaw, 1999.

———. Excerpt from "Our Image of Christ", *Iisus: Dve tysjači let religii i kul'tury*. Slavija, Interbook-business, 2001.

———. Excerpt from "Our Image of Christ", *Jezus 2000 let zgodovine vere in kulture*. Ljubljana, Slovenia: Druẑina, 2002.

———. "Tillit till Kyrkan." *Credo Katolsk Tidskrift* 4, no. 52 (1971): 168–74.

Acknowledgments

The correspondence between Ida Friederike Görres and Paulus Gordan, with abundant, detailed annotations by editor Hanna-Barbara Gerl-Falkovitz, and the detailed bibliography in Father Michael Kleinert's dissertation about Ida Görres were invaluable in preparing the translator's introduction.

Jan Bentz assisted in editing my translations of "Demolition Troops in the Church" and "Trusting the Church". Ann Aubrey Hanson and the talented team at Ignatius Press provided excellent copyediting. Any errors are my own.

I express my gratitude to Hochschule Heiligenkreuz in Austria, where I had the pleasure of being a visiting researcher while I was working on this translation. I extend a special thanks to the librarians of the combined library of the Hochschule and the Cistercian Abbey of Heiligenkreuz, who were unfailingly helpful.

This translation was made possible by a generous donation from Peter Thiel. Thank you, Peter.

Subject Index

Albertus Magnus, 86
Alfred the Great (English king), 181
Anselm of Canterbury, 118
aphasia, 109–10
Apocalypse, imagery of, 46
Apostles, faith of, 54–55
Arian heresy, 81, 91–92
Asch, Sholem, 61
Ascher, Jaakow Jizchak ben, 61
Asia, Christianity in, 66
Asmussen, Hans, 127
Auf dem Wege (Guardini), 118
Augustine of Hippo, 179–80
avatars, concept of, 59

Badenweiler, Germany, 30
Ball, Hugo, 111
Balthasar, Hans Urs von. *See* Von Balthasar, Hans Urs.
Bamboo Curtain, 66n30
beati possidentes (blessed are those who possess), 67
Benda, Julien, 82
Benedict XVI (Joseph Ratzinger), 11, 14–15, 22–23, 33–35, 183–87
Ben Hur (film), 60
Bergäcker Cemetery, Freiburg, Germany, 33
Bergengruen, Werner, 95–96
Bernanos, Georges, 105
"betrayal by the intellectuals", 82
Bible Movement, 97
"body of faith", 88–90
botanical analogies, 54–55, 78–79
Brentano, Clemens, 82
Breucha, Hermann, 178–79n20
Buber, Martin, 61
Byzantine Christianity (Ball), 111

Câmara, Hélder, 144
capacitas Dei (capacity for God), 105
capitalization of divine pronouns, 46
Catholic Church
  "body of faith", 88–90
  and celibacy, history of approaches to, 133–35
  Church, definitions and roles, 162–64
  Church history, 57–58, 164
  as City on the Hill, 12, 174, 180
  and faith, 108–13
  femininity and Mother Church, 138, 139–40
  future of, 174–77
  hope and optimism for, 12
  masculine emphasis, 138

Catholic Church (*continued*)
  memory, role of, 110
  non-practicing Catholics, 168
  orders, origins of, 57–58
  orthodox vocabulary, 71–72
  renewal movements, 97–98, 166–73
  secret unbelief within, 76
  self-cleansing of, 178
  suffering of, 178
  theological discussions within, nature of, 24–25
  trust in, 161–63
  twofold nature of, 163
  youth perspectives and roles, 74–76, 94
Catholic Church in crisis, 11–12, 20, 72–73, 75–76
  botanical analogies, 78–79
  contemporary state, and lack of trust, 151–62
  divisive issues, 72–73
  outcomes of challenges to, 173–82
  real estate development analogy, 79–81
  Second Vatican Council, legacy of, 77–79
  tradition, role in Church, 81–83
  youth perspectives, 74–76
Catholic Youth Movement, 13, 25, 79–80, 97–98, 134
celibacy
  contemporary approaches within the Church, 135–38
  contextual aspects, 29–30
  as dogma, 140–42
  and family life, 127–28
  femininity and Mother Church, 138, 139–40
  and gender roles, 138–39
  knowledge *per exclusionem*, 132
  opposition to, 121–24, 142–43
  potential of, 143–44
  and sacrifice, meaning of, 29n51, 125, 128–29
  theological objections to, 133–34
  viewed as prohibition, 124
chastity, 114–115
China, Christianity in, 66
Christ
  capitalization of "He", 46
  competing views and comprehensive pictures, 43–45, 48–49
  contemporary views of, 48–49, 62–64
  depicted as "Simple Man", 60–62
  fictional depictions of, 60
  His present ministry, 46–47
  historical evidence, 47
  humanity vs. dignity, 58–59, 61–63
  individual vs. holistic viewpoints, 49–50, 63–64
  "Life of Jesus" publications, 59–60
  life with, 64–65
  life without, 65–66
  and martyrs, 56–57
  Reality of the Lord, 53–54

reflected in the Church, 66–68
suffering of, 57
words of, 53
Christ: imagery of
artistic representations of, 60–61
image contrasted with person, 64–66
image of in Gospels, 51–53
images of, 45–46, 58–59, 64–66
in liturgical art, 56
Scriptural images, 47–48
Christopher, Saint, 114
Chrysostom, John, 141
Church. *See also* Catholic Church
Christians as minority group, 68–69
contrasted with Catholic Church, 50–51
early history, 54–55
ecumenical movements, 50–51, 50n6, 71
faith of, 108–9
Scripture, approaches to, 52–53
The Church in the Flesh (Görres), 17
Claudius, Matthias, 117
Cold War, 65–66
"com-munication", 40, 51
conversation, letters as, 18–19
"correspondence" as genre, 17–19
credo quia intelligum (I believe because I understand), 106
cultural revolution, 134n12

Das Geheimnis der Liebe (Asmussen), 127
deacons, 149
de Beauvoir, Simone, 30n52
de Foucauld, Charles, 62, 67
"Demolition Troops in the Church" (Görres), 11, 19–24, 71–83. *See also* Catholic Church in crisis
Dessauer, Philipp, 175
development, analogies for, 54–56, 81
Die Furche (Austrian newspaper), 28, 30
Die Presse (Viennese newspaper), 19–20, 21
Die Sendung (journal), 28
docilitas (teachability), 117
Dutch Catechism, 73

ecumenical movements. *See* Church
education, religious
for adults, 98
demand for, 98–99
Eichendorff, Joseph Freiherr von, 181
Emmerich, Anne Catherine, 26, 178
epistolary essays, 17–19
erotic feeling, 115–16
and celibacy, 122
Eucharist
belief in, 155
Christ's presence, 64
devaluation as "Lord's Supper", 137, 140
experimentation in the Church, 23

Eucharist (*continued*)
Home Masses, 174
Novus Ordo Mass, 23, 31
exegesis of Scripture, 46–47, 52–53
"exposed film" analogy, 55–56

faith
Benedict XVI on, 34–35
body of, 88–90
concreteness of, 89–90
confused with knowledge, 106–7
credo quia intelligum, 106
faith formation, 106–9
fides quarens intellectum, 119
hierarchy of truths, 85–87, 92–94
intellectus quaerens fidem, 118–19
religious duty vs. theory, 87–88
and Revelation, 108
sensus fidelium, 82, 91
tradition vs. "naked" theology, 90–92
truth, repressed, 90–91
truth and "body of faith", 88–90
"Faith: Skeleton or Body?" (Görres), 24–25, 85–94. *See also* faith
family life
parenthood, 126–28
and priesthood, 122–25
fanaticism, 105
Faulhaber, Michael von, 22
fides quaerens intellectum (faith seeking understanding), 106, 119
First Communion, 154
Foucauld, Charles de. *See* de Foucauld, Charles.
Freiburg, Germany, 33, 133
Fugel, Gebhard, 60
Futurism, Italian, 75

gender roles
abolition of the father, 138–39
emphasis within Church, 138
femininity and Mother Church, 138, 139–40
Görres' views, 30n52
masculine vs. feminine elements of Church, 138–40
rebellion against the mother, 138–39
women's roles, 30n52
generative power, 126–27
Gerl-Falkovitz, Hanna-Barbara, 26nn43–44
German language
Görres' use of, 36–38
and spelling, 39–40
Glaubenskörper, 88
gnosis, 106
God
faithfulness of, 33, 37, 176–77
passion for, 105
Goethe, Johann Wolfgang von, 59
Gordan, Paulus, 16, 20–22, 26–27, 31–33, 34

Görres, Albert, 135–36, 143
Görres, Carl-Josef, 14, 27
Görres, Ida Friederike
 background and life of, 13–15
 Benedict XVI, meeting with, 33–34
 Church, love for, 15
 controversial views, 22–23
 conversion experience, 13
 death and burial, 33
 eulogy for, 11, 14–15, 22–23, 33–35, 183–87
 independence, intellectual, 27
 on laity, 17–18
 pastoral sensitivity, 27
 published work, 15
 writing style, 130n9
Görres, Ida Friederike: correspondence of
 with Alfred Läpple, 34
 with Benedict XVI, 34–35
 with Paulus Gordan, 16, 20–22, 26–27, 31–33, 34
Gospels, 51–53
Guardini, Romano, 73–74, 118
Guitton, Jean, 81

Haecker, Theodor, 99
Heer, Friedrich, 71–72, 167
Hensel, Luise, 45n2
heresy, 58, 81–82, 165
The Hidden Face (Thérèse of Lisieux), 15
hierarchy of truths, 85–87
Hitler Youth, 170
Holy Spirit
 presence in Church, 82, 176
 signs of, 115
Humanae vitae (Paul VI), 160
Humani generis (Pius XII), 73
humility, 113–14, 116

Ignatius of Loyola, 57
imagery
 of Apocalypse, 46
 botanical analogies, 54–55, 78–79
 of Christ, 43–46, 48–49, 58–59, 64–66
 tree imagery, 132
 "winter" imagery, 34–35, 41
individuals, private judgment and faith, 106–7
Infant Jesus of Prague, 57
intellectus quaerens fidem (understanding seeking faith), 118–19
intuition, 54
Iron Curtain, 65–66
Is Celibacy Outdated? (Görres), 28
Italian Futurism, 75

Jesus the Young Man (Scharrelmann), 60
John XXIII, 166
Jung, C. G., 140
Jünger, Ernest, 173

Kierkegaard, Søren, 112
knowledge
 confused with faith, 106–7
 exclusion and knowing, 132
 gnosis, 106
Kulturkampf, 134
Küng, Hans, 34

language
  Görres' use of, 36–38
  martial language, 20, 71, 167
  and spelling, 39–40
Läpple, Alfred, 34
laypersons
  faith of, 81–82, 87–88
  hidden saints, 179
  isolation and fear, 32
  lay theology, 95–97, 99–100, 105–6
  and priestly duties, 149–50
  "revaluation" of natural Christian life, 136–37
  theological vs. religious interests, 95–97
"A Letter on the Church" (Görres), 17, 22
letters and correspondence as genre, 17–19
Lewis, C. S., 39, 52, 74, 99, 116, 117
Little King of Grace (Petit Roi de la Gloire), 57
Liturgical Movement, 97, 134
liturgy
  and Christ's ministry, 46
  liturgical reform, 156–57
Lorenz, Konrad, 71

The Man Born to Be King (Sayers), 59–60
marriage, 124–25. *See also* family life
martial language. *See* warfare and martial language
martyrs, 56–57
Mary, devotion to, 58, 62, 140
masculinity. *See* gender roles
Mass. *See* Eucharist
memory, role of, 109–10
Michael the Archangel, 20
Mission and Grace: Essays in Pastoral Theology, 146
Möhler, Johann Adam, 49–50, 88, 110–11, 113, 133
More, Thomas, 177
motherhood. *See* gender roles
Mottke the Vagabond (Asch), 61

National Socialism, 169–70
nature
  botanical analogies, 54–55, 78–79
  descriptions of, 24
  rehabilitation of, 134
  tree imagery, 132
Neue Freie Presse (newspaper), 21
Newman, John Henry, 81–82, 89, 101, 106–7, 151, 152
New Order of the Mass, 23, 31
"Nicodemic" strategy, 71–72, 167
Nietzsche, Friedrich, 76, 78
Nigg, Walter, 155
"non-practicing" Catholics, 168
Novus Ordo Mass, 23, 31

"On the Doctor and the Sick" (Volk), 102
opinion, 68
Origen, 182
Ortega y Gasset, José, 153
orthography used in text, 39–40
"Our Image of Christ: A Letter" (Görres), 17–19, 43–69. *See also* Christ; Christ: imagery of

parenthood, 127–28. *See also* family life
"The Parish Priest" (Rahner), 146
Pascal, Blaise, 99
passion for God, 105
"pedagogical fraud", 100
Perelandra (Lewis), 74
photography and "exposed film" analogy, 55–56
piety, 116–17
plant analogies, 54–55, 78–79
poverty, guilt regarding, 67
priesthood
  and gender roles, 138–39
  misunderstandings of, 144–49
  mystery of, 141, 147
  part-time, possibility of, 29, 144–45, 149
  privileges of priests, 100
  shortage of priests, 149–50
prophecy vs. theology, 112–13
public opinion, 68

Rahner, Hugo, 139, 182
Rahner, Karl, 59, 146
The Rambler (periodical), 81
Ratzinger, Joseph. *See* Benedict XVI (Joseph Ratzinger)
real estate development analogy, 79–81
religion, nature of, 103–4
religious experience, 116
"Remarks on Celibacy" (Görres), 28–30, 121–50. *See also* celibacy
"reverence syndrome", 103–4, 105, 117
Rheinischer Merkur (German newspaper), 28
Rosenberg, Alfons, 18
Rosenstock-Huessy, Eugen, 81, 83

sacraments, 154–55
sacrifice, 29n51, 125, 128–29
saints
  hidden, 179
  lives of, 15
sanctity, 15
Satanism, 105
Sayers, Dorothy, 59–60
Schott Missal, 116
Schulmeister, Otto, 21
Schurr, Viktor, 26
scientific method, 138
Scripture exegesis, 46–47, 52–53
The Second Sex (Beauvoir), 30n52
Second Vatican Council, 23, 30–31, 77–79, 136–37, 166
Seewald, Peter, 23, 34
sensus fidelium (religious instinct of the faithful), 82, 91
Sermon on the Mount, 173
sexuality
  Catholic sexual mythology, 135–36
  erotic feeling, 115–16, 122
  generative power, 126–27
  sexual revolution, 29n51
Song of Songs, 47
spelling used in text, 39–40
spirituality
  and chastity, 114–15

spirituality (*continued*)
individual striving for, 104–6
use of term, 87
"Spirituality of Studying Theology" (Görres), 24–27, 95–119. *See also* theology
Stern, Karl, 138
St. Ulrich, Bollschweil, Germany, 26–27
suffering of the Church, 178
Synod of Würzburg, 33

Teilhard de Chardin, Pierre, 62–63, 112, 141, 142n19, 166
Ten Commandments, 153
Teresa of Calcutta, 166–67
theology. *See also* faith; spirituality
disposition of theology students, 102–3
faith confused with knowledge, 106–7
faith formation, 106–9
humility vs. vanity, 113–14
lay aptitude for, 105–6
lay interest, theological vs. religious, 95–97
lay theology, 99–100
as male element, 139
as map, 45–46, 48–50
"naked" theology, 90
piety and love, 116–17
priestly roles, 100
role of memory, 111–12
theologians, attributes of, 116–17
theology, lay aptitude for, 105–6
theology study, entrance to for laypersons, 118–19
university education in theology, 100–102
Thérèse of Lisieux, 15
Third Reich, 158
National Socialism, 169–70
Thorvaldsen, Bertel, 60
trahison des clercs (betrayal by the intellectuals), 82
transformative power of celibacy, 129–30
translator's methodology
chapter outlines, 16–33
spelling, 39–40
use of language, 35–38
tree imagery, 132
"Trusting the Church" (Görres), 30–33, 151–82, 185–86
Truth
biographical order of, 92–93
and "body of faith", 88–90
hierarchy of truths, 85–87, 92–94
repressed, 90–91
tzaddikim (righteous ones), 61

unbelief
private judgment as root of, 106–7
secret unbelief, 76
Under the Sun of Satan (Bernanos), 105
university education, 100–101

vanity, 114
Vatican II. *See* Second Vatican Council
virginity, 30, 130–31, 141–42. *See also* celibacy

Volk, Georg, 102
Von Balthasar, Hans Urs, 21–22, 26
Von Hügel, Friedrich, 99
Von Speyr, Adrienne, 21

warfare and martial language, 20, 71, 72, 167
waste, culture of, 74–75
"We are the Church" slogan, 73–74
Werfel, Franz, 61
"winter" imagery, 34–35, 41
women. *See* gender roles
Wort und Wahrheit (journal), 21

Youth Movement, 13, 25, 79–80, 97–98, 134, 184

Zagorin, Perez, 72n3

Scripture Index

Old Testament

Genesis

1:28, 128n4
18:1–33, 176n17
19:1–3, 176n17

Exodus

17:6, 176n18

Numbers

6, 65n29
20:1–13, 176n18

Judges

6:11–24, 176n17
13:1–25, 176n17

1 Kings

17:6, 176n17

Psalms

22:1, 46n3
68:19, 130n9
78:15, 176n18
105:41, 176n18
147, 180n22

Wisdom

1:4, 115n20

Isaiah

40:4, 80n16
42:3, 173n10
58:11–12, 83n21

New Testament

Matthew

12:20, 173n10
13:16–17, 67n31
13:24–29, 77n13
13:24–30, 87n1, 173n10
13:33, 141n16
22:30, 129n8
23:4, 122n1
24:36, 175n13
26:26, 110n11

Mark

3:13, 65n28
3:25, 73n5
13:33, 55n13

Luke

1:68, 184n1
13:18–21, 93n4
20:36, 129n7
22:19, 110n11

John

3:30, 38, 94n5
4:34, 130n9
10:28–29, 176n16
14:26, 108n9

Romans

3:25, 54n11, 64n27, 69n32

1 Corinthians

7, 51n7
13:12, 112n17

2 Corinthians

11:2, 51n7

Galatians

5:16–26, 115n21
6:2, 130n9

Ephesians

2:19, 132n10
5:3–18, 115n21
6:12, 175n15

Colossians

1:15–16, 46

Hebrews

1:3, 46
13:2, 176n17
13:8, 51n8

James

1:17, 146n23

1 John

3:2, 37, 69n33
3:16, 129n6
5:20, 46

Revelation

1:5, 57n15
1:12–20, 46n4
5:6, 46n4
6:2, 46n4
19:11–15, 46n4